D0940585

WARBIRDS
AROUND THE WORLD

JOHN KING

WARBIRD PHOTOGRAPHS BY
JOHN KING • PHILIP MAKANNA • GORDON BAIN

Airlife
England

JOHN KING has held a private pilot's licence for more than 30 years and has been involved in professional journalism and air-to-air photography for almost as long. He is presently regarded as New Zealand's foremost aviation photographer and is editor of *New Zealand Sport Flying* magazine. John has had six books published, including *Wings Over New Zealand*, and is a regular contributor to magazines in several countries.

Photograph: Michael King

GORDON BAIN is an aviation professional as well as a specialist photographer and author. His books include *De Havilland: a Pictorial Tribute*, the definitive work on that illustrious British manufacturer, and he is currently working on his fourth title. Based in Sussex, England, Gordon travels extensively to Europe and the USA in search of material for his camera and word processor.

Photograph: Malcolm Blows

PHILIP MAKANNA has been photographing restored World War 2 aircraft around the world since he first saw a Confederate Air Force show in 1974. He lives in San Francisco, California, and is the author of books *Ghosts: A Time Remembered* and *Ghosts: Vintage Aircraft of World War II* as well as the creator of the well-known *Ghosts* calendars.

Photograph: Ken Morley

© 1999 John King

First published in the UK in 2000 by Airlife Publishing Ltd

First Published in New Zealand by Saint Publishing Ltd

British Library Cataloguing-in-Publication Data
   A catalogue record for this book is available from the British Library

ISBN 1 84037 169 2

The information in this book is true and complete to the best of our knowledge. All recommendations are made without any guarantee on the part of the Publisher, who also disclaims any liability incurred in connection with the use of this data or specific details.

All rights reserved. No part of this book may be reproduced or transmitted in any form or by any means, electronic or mechanical including photocopying, recording or by any information storage and retrieval system, without permission from the Publisher in writing.

Printed in Hong Kong

Airlfe Publishing Ltd
101 Longden Road, Shrewsbury, SY3 9EB, England
Email: airlife@airlifebooks.com
Website: www.airlifebooks.com

Front Cover: The Confederate Air Force's P-51D Mustang *Gunfighter* is a currently flying example of one of the most successful fighters of World War 2. *Philip Makanna*

Back Cover: Bearcat and Corsair fighters line the deck of USS *Midway* in April 1949, ready for takeoff. *Parker Mudge*

Title Page: de Havilland DH115 Vampire.

Opposite: Consolidated B-24 Liberator over California. *Gordon Bain*

Page 4-5: Hawker Sea Fury. *Gordon Bain*

CONTENTS

AVRO 631 CADET

This Avro 626 with its third cockpit for gunnery training is the RNZAF's only surviving example of any of its prewar aircraft. Wg Cdr John Lanham, seen here near Auckland, flew it briefly before it was retired as a static museum exhibit. *John King*

A.V. Roe, the company and the man, go right back to the very origins of British aviation. Alliott Verdon Roe began aircraft design in 1906 and three years later was the first Briton to fly an all-British aeroplane. The Avro company was formed in 1911 and its first major product was the 504, a trainer designed in 1912. Output over almost 20 years ran to a total of more than 8000, and the RAF still operated impressed civil Avro 504Ns in 1940 as glider tugs.

Avro production from 1915 was a series of biplanes, with the odd throwback to Roe's earliest triplane endeavours, some military but mostly civil aircraft. A few were large airliners and led to the Fokker F.VIIB/3m being built under licence as the Avro 618 Ten (after the number of occupants), but the company became best known worldwide for its Avian series of light open-cockpit sporting biplanes. They coincided with the period of long-distance record breaking, and Bert Hinkler used an Avro 581 Avian in 1928 to become the first pilot to fly solo from England to Australia. Production quantities never matched those of the contemporary Moths, but the Avian was light and pleasant to fly.

The same qualities extended to the military trainers which followed. The Avro 621 Tutor of 1929, a 504 replacement, set the trend in welded steel-tube fuselage structure for all subsequent models and had a 155 hp Armstrong Siddeley Mongoose IIIA radial engine. Almost 400 were made for the RAF and a few European air forces, plus 57 in South Africa. They were followed by the bigger and more powerful Avro 626 Prefect, an all-purpose trainer seating two but with three cockpits, the rear one fitted with a ring for gunnery work.

Smaller and more economical than the Tutor was the Avro 631 Cadet, powered by a 135 hp Armstrong Siddeley Genet Major and made for the civil training schools which wanted a robust trainer with similar flying characteristics. Only 36 were built before the 631 was replaced by the 643 with raised rear seat for better visibility, and after eight of those came the 643 Mk II Cadet with its 150 hp Genet Major IA mounted further forward. More than half the production of 61 Mk IIs went to the RAAF and it is a popular vintage aeroplane in Australia today.

The cost of the Genet Major engine compared to the DH Gipsy Major, plus the lack of folding wings which called for more hangar space, limited the appeal of the 631 to the private owner. Cost and impeccable handling qualities lost it the major RAF trainer contract which went to the cheaper DH82A Tiger Moth with its more quirky characteristics, thought to be better for teaching service pilots how to fly. The biggest operator was Air Service Training, Hamble, which used a total of 17 black-and-silver 631s, 11 of them still active at the outbreak of war in 1939.

The Irish Air Corps operated Avro 621 Tutors, but its pilots considered them underpowered and unsuccessful. Nevertheless, six Avro 631 Cadets were delivered to Ireland in March 1932 as C1 to C6, painted in the IAC colours of black fuselage and silver wings with the national colours in stripes across the wings and tail. They were popular and served for many years

• Avro 631 Cadet	
Manufacturer:	A.V. Roe Ltd
Type:	Two-seat primary trainer
Engine:	One Armstrong Siddeley Genet Major I 7-cylinder radial, air cooled, 135 hp
Wingspan:	30 ft ....9.14 m
Length:	24 ft 9 in ....7.54 m
Height:	8 ft 9 in ....2.67 m
Empty weight:	1180 lb ....535 kg
Max loaded:	1900 lb ....862 kg
Max range:	350 miles ....563 km
Max speed:	118 mph ....190 km/h
First flight:	October 1931
In production:	1932-1934

until replaced by Miles Magisters, but all except one have faded from the scene.

C3 crashed in August 1932 and the IAC ordered a replacement from the Avro factory. Production of the 643 Cadet had taken the earlier model's place and making another 631 proved slightly awkward, but C7, number seven of the original six, was duly delivered in December 1934. It was later sold into private hands but met with a mishap in 1946, standing on its nose and damaging the engine and forward fuselage. C7 languished for years before being rescued from Ireland and restoration started in England, then it was brought to New Zealand where the work was completed over a number of years. Only two Avro 631s are left in the world, one on static display in a Portuguese museum and one flying out of Auckland's North Shore, New Zealand.

Jim Schmidt test flies his newly-restored ex-Irish Air Corps Avro 631 north of Auckland, New Zealand, in January 1999, more than 50 years after its previous flight. *John King*

BOEING STEARMAN MODEL 75

Steve Bicknell's PT-17 shows the USAAC blue-and-yellow colour scheme, Recently imported as New Zealand's fourth example, it spent most of its life in Florida but was restored to flying condition in Nova Scotia. *John King*

Lloyd Stearman had a strong influence in American light aviation from the early 1920s, and was unusual in having his name on an aircraft produced by a major manufacturer. Already known with Laird in Chicago and as chief mechanic with the Swallow Airplane Manufacturing Company, Stearman tried to persuade Swallow to use the steel-tube airframe developed some years earlier in Detroit, but the company's refusal led to his and test pilot Walter Beech's resignations.

The two of them joined forces with Clyde Cessna in 1924 and set up the Travel Air Manufacturing Company in Wichita, Kansas, concentrating on two-passenger and mail biplanes. Cessna left in 1927 as he wanted to build monoplanes, and Stearman formed the Stearman Aircraft Company in Venice, California, around the Lyle-Hoyt Aircraft Corporation, formerly Travel Air's West Coast distributor. The factory soon moved to Wichita, making three-seaters, trainers and mailplanes, and became part of the United Aircraft and Transport Corporation which formed in 1929.

The massive United group grew out of early expansion of Boeing, which had started as an aircraft manufacturer in Seattle, Washington, in 1916. During the 1920s Boeing accumulated airlines, engine (Pratt & Whitney) and propeller (Hamilton Standard) companies, a Vancouver shipyard and other aircraft builders such as Chance Vought and Sikorsky. All operated independently but without duplication, and all used one another's products where possible, under United Airlines' overall management unit. They were in trouble during the Depression, however, and the Air Mail Act of 1934 banned any one company from owning both manufacturing and commercial airline operating interests.

The Boeing Airplane Company split off entirely, with Stearman as a wholly-owned subsidiary. In April 1939 Stearman became the Wichita Division of the Boeing Aircraft Company, although it continued to design and build aircraft under its own designation. When the B-29 programme called for a new factory at Wichita it became the division's Plant 2, with the original Stearman facility known as Plant 1.

Stearman's Model 70 appeared in 1934 and won a military primary trainer competition. Of the 8584 examples of the open-cockpit tandem two-seat Model 70 to Model 76 series, plus another 1762 sets of components as spares, most were made after Stearman had become Boeing's Wichita Division, but the name stuck.

They were made for the US Navy as the NS and N2S, the US Army Air Corps as the PT-13, PT-17, PT-18 and PT-27, and they were exported to several South American countries as well as Britain, China and, after World War 2, the Philippines. Engines came from Jacobs, Continental and Lycoming, usually in the 220 to 225 hp range but including a batch of 420 hp Pratt & Whitney R-985s for the Philippine Constabulary. The Canadians called it the Kaydet and it became the standard trainer of North America, the equivalent of the earlier British Avro 504 and contemporary Tiger Moth, or the German Jüngmann and Bestmann. Countless thousands of army and navy airmen learned to fly on this superb trainer, big,

strong, forgiving and kindly but responding well to the right technique.

Such qualities ensured the Stearman's postwar survival, and in 1950 almost half the original production was still on the US civil register, with more than 2000 still in service in 1959, mostly as crop dusters. Many were re-engined with 450 hp Pratt & Whitneys to carry more load, and some have even been seen with 600 hp Wasp engines, modified as the ultimate in aerobatic display aircraft.

Today they no longer have to carry agricultural chemicals to justify their existence, and the classic Stearman biplane is a sought-after sporting warbird. It may be far from over-powered with its original 220 hp radial engine, but its handling qualities endear it to continuing generations of new pilots, 65 years after it first came off the drawing board.

Being painted for visibility as trainers and not camouflaged, Stearmans are invariably colourful. The US Navy yellow scheme is shown by the pair flown by Jack Sadler and Ernie Persich out of Madera, California. *Philip Makanna*

• Boeing Stearman PT-17A	
Manufacturer:	Boeing Aircraft Company
Type:	Two-seat primary trainer
Engine:	One Continental R-670-5 7-cylinder radial, air cooled, 220 hp
Wingspan:	32 ft 2 in ......9.8 m
Length:	24 ft 1 in ......7.32 m
Height:	9 ft 2 in ......2.8 m
Empty weight:	1936 lb ......878 kg
Max loaded:	2717 lb ......1232 kg
Max range:	505 miles ......813 km
Max speed:	124 mph ......200 km/h at sea level
First flight:	December 1933
In production:	1934-1945

CAC CA-25 Winjeel

Apart from the larger-diameter engine, outward-facing axles and larger canopy to cover three occupants, the Winjeel bears an uncanny resemblance to the contemporary Provost developed on the other side of the world. This Winjeel is one of two in New Zealand.
John King

The Commonwealth Aircraft Corporation (CAC) was formed at Fishermens Bend, Victoria, in 1936 as the basis of an independent Australian aircraft manufacturing industry. It took over Tugan Aircraft Ltd and especially the services of Wing Commander L.J. (later Sir Lawrence) Wackett.

The company had a long history of aircraft production, under licence and of its own designs. First was the CA-1 Wirraway, a local development of the North American NA-33 advanced trainer which sported twin forward-firing machine guns and a single gun on a swivel mount in the rear cockpit, as well as strengthened wings and tail for dive bombing. Without any teeth but able to carry practice bombs was the CA-6 Wackett trainer, an intermediate step between the Tiger Moth and Wirraway and powered by a 175 hp Warner Scarab radial engine. Wartime production included the Boomerang fighter, an indigenous design produced very quickly by making some 65 per cent of its airframe parts in common with the Wirraway, and the CA-18 Mustang, licence-built and first delivered to the RAAF in June 1945.

In 1948 the RAAF saw the need to replace both the Tiger Moth and Wirraway, showing signs of age and wear, with a single trainer which could be used from *ab initio* flying right up to advanced stage. The technical specification called for simple but robust construction, economical operation and seating for three, and CAC's response was the Winjeel, the Aboriginal word for young eagle. Two prototypes were built as CA-22s, powered by the readily available 450 hp Pratt & Whitney R-985 Wasp Junior and first flown in February 1951.

Testing was prolonged by several factors, not least among them the company's major redesign and licensed production of the CA-27 Sabre, together with its Rolls-Royce Avon engine. Nor did the Winjeel at first meet RAAF specifications, particularly in spinning which is always a necessary feature of service aircraft. Changes to the size and position of the fin and rudder finally induced it to spin, and other major modifications resulted in its final acceptance, with Government approval for the production of 62 Winjeels coming in September 1953. The first definitive CA-25 flew 18 months later.

Plans were made to fit the indigenous CAC Cicada 450 hp radial engine in the 31st and subsequent airframes, but the entire production flew with Pratt & Whitney power. In appearance the Winjeel was remarkably similar to the contemporary Hunting Percival P.56 Provost which, although fractionally smaller, was heavier and powered by a 550 hp Alvis Leonides and became the standard RAF two-seat trainer of the 1950s.

Winjeels began to be replaced as the RAAF's basic trainers by New Zealand-made CT-4 Airtrainers from the mid-1970s, but they stayed in service until the final four were auctioned off in October 1995 – two years after the bulk of their CT-4 replacements had themselves been sold. In the latter period Winjeels were used by operational conversion units for Mirage pilots and also on forward air control prac-

tice with No. 76 Squadron, being seen all over Australia for more than 25 years on training missions and taking part in airshows.

During a service life spanning 40 years only 15 Winjeels were written off in accidents. Some are still gate guardians, instructional airframes or museum exhibits, but most of the remainder have been sold to private owners and nearly 20 are airworthy.

As a warbird the CA-25 Winjeel is in demand in its native Australia and two have filtered across the Tasman Sea to New Zealand. They are recognised as useful aeroplanes, fun to fly and making the right radial engine noises.

Painted as a forward air control Winjeel, A85-445 was in fact retired from the RAAF in 1975 before the type's FAC role, then sat unused for some years before the Australian authorities allowed the private use of ex-military aircraft. It was shipped to New Zealand in 1994 and is owned by John Mathewson who flies it here over the Maniototo region of Central Otago. *John King*

• CAC CA-25 Winjeel	
Manufacturer:	Commonwealth Aircraft Corporation
Type:	Three-seat basic trainer
Engine:	One Pratt & Whitney R-985-AN-2 Wasp Junior 9-cylinder radial, air cooled, 445 hp
Wingspan:	38 ft 9 in ...... 11.81 m
Length:	29 ft 4½ in ...... 8.92 m
Height:	8 ft 3 in ...... 2.52 m
Empty weight:	3240 lb ...... 1471 kg
Max loaded:	4235 lb ...... 1923 kg
Endurance:	5 hr 30 min
Max speed:	186 mph ...... 299 km/h
First flight:	3 February 1951
In production:	1955-1957

DE HAVILLAND DH82A TIGER MOTH

Tiger Moths are often used for joyriding, such as Biplane Adventures' ZK-BCO, painted in a postwar RNZAF scheme, with Tom Middleton at the controls near its Wanaka base. *Philip Makanna*

In British countries the most familiar trainer, at least in the eye of the public, is the Tiger Moth. It also epitomises the vintage biplane, not least because it has survived in greater numbers than any other type where World War 2 pilots were taught to fly as part of the Empire Flying Training Scheme. It has even found its way in some numbers into the USA, the home of the much more substantial equivalent, the Stearman.

Even in its heyday, from 1939 until 1945 when the need for new pilots was suddenly reduced, the Tiger Moth was something of an anachronism. Delicate in appearance with slender lines, rudimentary in its instruments, with no flaps or wheel brakes and steered only by means of a tailskid, it nevertheless was demanding enough that pupils who first encountered the Tiger Moth learned the basics and could go on to greater things. Military aircraft were almost invariably fast monoplanes with enclosed cockpits and increasingly complex systems, but still the British pilot's first encounter with aviation was an open-cockpit biplane with its origins firmly in the 1920s.

The Tiger Moth was part of the family of light aircraft started by Geoffrey de Havilland in 1925 with the DH60 Moth, a two-seat open-cockpit wood-and-fabric biplane. Six years later the DH60 had spawned several variants, including one with steel tube fuselage and inverted Gipsy III engine of 120 hp which was offered to the Air Ministry in Great Britain as a military basic trainer. While it was popular with the RAF, instructors said that access to the front cockpit, surrounded by centre-section struts and with the top wing and fuel tank a couple of feet overhead, was less than adequate for somebody wearing a parachute.

Arthur Hagg, de Havilland's chief designer, dismantled a DH60MIII Moth and rearranged the top wings, moving the centre section forward, clear of the cockpit, and sweeping all wings back to maintain the centre of lift. The result was different enough to be given the new type number of DH82 and, although it was not perfect in that the wings no longer folded and the ribs were not parallel to the airflow, the Tiger Moth became the standard basic trainer. Powered by 130 hp of Gipsy Major, it won acceptance over the Avro 631 Cadet and Hawker Tomtit because of its ease of maintenance and slightly more difficult handling characteristics, thought to be good for teaching the basics of flying.

More than 8000 were made between 1932 and the end of World War 2. English wartime production was moved to Morris Motors to make room for Mosquitos at the de Havilland factory, and Tiger Moths were also built in Canada, Australia, New Zealand, Portugal, Norway and Sweden. Military pilots learned to fly them in many British Commonwealth countries before progressing to Harvards and then on to service aircraft.

The attrition rate was high in those hectic days of training, especially before they were painted yellow for visibility, but the instructor and pupil survival rate was high. But especially in Australia and New Zealand, the postwar life of the Tiger Moth was much harder than mere flying training. Cheap and available in large numbers, they were used to pioneer the fledgling aerial agricultural industry, carrying fertiliser in hoppers fitted into their front cockpits to be dropped on the landscape and transform large areas into viable pasture. They were utterly unsuited to the job, but nevertheless performed nobly until their role was taken over by aircraft specifically designed for the purpose.

Today the DH82A Tiger Moth has a much more gentle life as a vintage biplane in private ownership.

• de Havilland DH82A Tiger Moth	
Manufacturer:	The de Havilland Aircraft Company
Type:	Two-seat primary trainer
Engine:	One de Havilland Gipsy Major 1 4-cylinder inverted, air cooled, 130 hp
Wingspan:	29 ft 4 in ... 8.94 m
Length:	23 ft 11 in ... 7.3 m
Height:	8 ft 9½ in ... 2.7 m
Empty weight:	1115 lb ... 506 kg
Max loaded:	1825 lb ... 828 kg
Max range:	285 miles ... 459 km
Max speed:	109 mph ... 175 km/h at sea level
First flight:	26 October 1931
In production:	1932-1945

Tom Newland, flying his Auckland-based Tiger Moth, is an old hand at this. At the beginning of World War 2 he signed up for the Fleet Air Arm as a way to get into flying early, but on the way to England his ship was intercepted by a German raider and sunk soon after leaving New Zealand. He and his colleagues were put ashore on a Pacific island after signing an agreement not to take up arms against Germany. They were rescued and repatriated, the New Zealand Government honoured the agreement and he spent his entire war instructing on Tiger Moths. *John King*

DE HAVILLAND DH94 MOTH MINOR

John King

When Geoffrey (later Sir Geoffrey) de Havilland introduced his new Moth to the British aviation public in 1925 he set a trend. Here was a light biplane, with wooden structure and covered with fabric for easy repairs, carrying two people in tandem open cockpits on the modest power of a 60 hp Cirrus engine. It quickly caught on to the extent that the Moth name became synonymous with light aeroplanes throughout the British Empire.

The Moth's origins date from 1923 as a combination of ideas from both the DH51 biplane and DH53 Humming Bird monoplane. The two- or three-seat DH51 was an early attempt to produce a simple and cheap aircraft, but engine developments pushed up the price and only three were made. Entered in the 1923 *Daily Mail*-sponsored light aircraft trials at Lympne, Kent, the DH53 flew well enough, but de Havilland realised the limited potential of the type, restricted by rules keeping the engine size under 1100 cc, would not progress the cause of aviation. His re-thinking resulted in the DH60, smaller than the DH51 but capable of development.

The American equivalent of an aeroplane for large numbers of future pilots to learn in and enjoy flying would be the Piper Cub of the following decade, but the Moth had one major marketing advantage.

British countries were scattered around the globe, as yet unconnected by airways, and many young aviators (and aviatrixes – such women as Jean Batten and Amy Johnson were upsetting male dominance) were willing to fly solo in their open Moths in search of distance and time records, or sometimes just to return home from Britain. Over the following decade or so the headlines and column inches of newspaper reports describing their Moths and their adventures added up to a marketer's dream.

More Moths followed, not only more powerful engines in the DH60 series but also new monoplanes and other biplanes. Most of the Moth family had enclosed cabins and the 130 hp Gipsy Major which became the ubiquitous British light aircraft engine of the 1930s and well into the 1950s. Some were operated by air forces in British countries, particularly those smaller nations which could afford only the most modest of aircraft.

In 1937 the Moth wheel turned full circle. Long gone was the original Moth idea of light weight but reasonable performance on modest power, but the new DH94 Moth Minor marked a return to first principles, even if it was a radical departure in being a low-wing monoplane. Still, its all-wood construction stayed with trusty de Havilland methods and it sat two in tandem, either in open cockpits or covered by a neat coupé top, and the whole ensemble was given a performance similar to the Tiger Moth's but with only 90 hp from the new Gipsy Minor engine. A perforated air brake hinged under the centre section took care of the glide angle for approach, the wings folded for easy hangarage, and a tendency for the spin to flatten, which caused test pilots John Cunningham and Geoffrey de Havilland Junior to abandon the prototype and take to their parachutes, was cured by raising the tailplane.

By mid-1939 Moth Minor production was eight per week and examples were exported to Australia, Canada, New Zealand and South Africa. In early 1940, however, after 74 had been made at the Hatfield

de Havilland DH94 Moth Minor		
Manufacturer:	The de Havilland Aircraft Company	
Type:	Two-seat primary trainer	
Engine:	One de Havilland Gipsy Minor 4–cylinder inverted, air cooled, 90 hp	
Wingspan:	36 ft 7 in	11.15 m
Length:	24 ft 5 in	7.44 m
Height:	6 ft 4 in	1.93 m
Empty weight:	983 lb	446 kg
Max loaded:	1550 lb	703 kg
Max range:	300 miles	483 km
Max speed:	118 mph	190 km/h
First flight:	22 June 1937	
In production:	1938-1942	

factory, production was stopped to make way for the war effort. All the drawings, tools, jigs and remaining components and partly built aircraft were shipped to the Australian de Havilland factory at Bankstown, Sydney, where a further 41 were completed, but only two were made from scratch.

All Bankstown production was for the RAAF as an interim trainer until the Australian Tiger Moth line was brought up to full capacity, supplemented by impressed Moth Minors imported prewar. The type was also impressed into RAF and RNZAF use as light trainers and general communications aircraft, and almost all of the DH94s active today have had military use early in their careers.

With its long wings which fold from the centre section, the Moth Minor is both aerodynamically efficient and frugal of hangar space, marking a return to the original concept of de Havilland's Moth series. ZK-AKM was imported into New Zealand prewar from Australia and saw service with the RNZAF. Owned and flown by Stan and Gilly Smith at Auckland's North Shore airfield, it is one of the world's few DH94s currently airworthy. *John King*

DE HAVILLAND CANADA DHC-1 CHIPMUNK

Gordon Bain

The de Havilland Canada plant was established at Downsview, Ontario, in 1928 to assemble Cirrus Moths. In 1937, with a solid record of developing de Havilland products for local conditions, general manager Phil Garratt was successful in his bid to have DH Canada established as a manufacturer in its own right. During the war years the factory produced more than 3000 aircraft, particularly Tiger Moths, Ansons and Mosquitoes.

Ideas of postwar production started taking shape in 1943, with the Mosquito project entirely under Canadian government control. While the Fox Moth was a popular bush aeroplane and could be further adapted, the company saw that a larger, rugged and purpose-built aircraft was needed and, with its direct experience in the field, wanted to undertake all aspects of design and production. The parent company in England, however, thought that was slightly ambitious and suggested that a postwar trainer replacement for the Tiger Moth would be more appropriate as an initial engineering exercise with a wider market.

Work started in 1945 on a two-seat trainer, the DHC-1, as the first in the company's series of indigenous designs and called the Chipmunk after a decision to name them all after Canadian animals. A prime requirement was enclosed seating, Canadian winters being far from conducive to pleasant flying in open cockpits. Indeed, the local Tiger Moth production had long been provided with a sliding canopy, cabin heater, brakes, tailwheel and other refinements to make it a more practical trainer.

Leading the Chipmunk team was Doug Hunter, originally from the DH works at Stag Lane, London, but staying in Canada following the Mosquito project. The design was largely the work of Wsiewolod J. ("Jacki") Jakimiuk. A refugee from the 1939 German invasion of Poland, where he had been designing PZL fighters as chief engineer at the National Aircraft Factory in Warsaw, he then joined the French National Aeronautical Corporation before going to de Havilland Canada as chief designer at the fall of France.

The first Chipmunk was test flown in May 1946, only five months after the production of two prototypes was authorised, and was shipped to England a few months later. In general outline very similar to the prewar Moth Minor with its elegantly tapered wings and trademark DH fin and rudder, it nevertheless marked a complete departure from the usual de Havilland construction methods of wood and steel tube, covered in fabric. The new postwar trainer still had fixed tailwheel undercarriage but had an all-metal stressed skin fuselage, and the single-spar low wing had a stressed skin leading edge and was fabric covered aft of the spar. A sliding canopy covered the two occupants seated in tandem, and with its excellent harmony of controls and general handling response the Chipmunk soon became highly popular. Power was by no means excessive and was provided by a 145 hp uprated version of the Gipsy Major.

Canadian Chipmunk output at Downsview reached a total of 218 and another 60 were made in Portugal, but the main production was in the de Havilland factories in England, 111 at Hatfield and 889 at Chester. The DHC-1 was also available as a civil trainer, although it was more expensive than its contemporaries – especially war-surplus Tiger Moths – and was found in some numbers with aero clubs in Australia. Most, however, saw military service with

several air forces, and now that almost all military examples have been retired after some 50 years of teaching students and new entrants to fly they are finding their way into private civil hands.

The Chipmunk may lack such touring necessities as luggage space and fuel endurance, but its attractive lines and handling qualities endear it to a new breed of civil pilots. Even allowing for a natural attrition rate, the nearly 1300 made in three countries should ensure its continued presence in the skies of many countries for years to come.

• de Havilland Canada DHC-1 Chipmunk		
Manufacturer:	........The de Havilland Aircraft of Canada Ltd	
Type:	.....................Two-seat primary trainer	
Engine:	....................One de Havilland Gipsy Major 10 Mk 2 4-cylinder inverted, air cooled, 145 hp	
Wingspan:	.............34 ft 4 in	................10.47 m
Length:	...................25 ft 5 in	................7.82 m
Height:	...................7 ft	..........................2.13 m
Empty weight:	........1425 lb	....................655 kg
Max loaded:	..........2100 lb	....................990 kg
Max range:	.............280 miles	................470 km
Max speed:	.............137 mph	.................220 km/h at sea level
First flight:	.............22 May 1946	
In production:	1947-1958	

Although Chipmunks have always been rare in New Zealand, recent military retirements in England and India have seen a recent influx of the type. Seen here over Lake Ellesmere near Christchurch in February 1998 is a quartet of Chipmunks flown by Peter Hendriks (front), Jim Lawson, Jim Chapman and Lou McAllister. *John King*

MILES M.14A MAGISTER

Gordon Bain

Phillips & Powis Aircraft produced a range of pleasant and useful light monoplane aircraft during the 1930s, all made of plywood and usually powered by the ubiquitous British engine, the 130 hp de Havilland Gipsy Major. Among them was the Miles M.2 Hawk Major, an open-cockpit two-seat trainer intended for aero club use and fitted with comprehensive equipment for the time, including vacuum-operated flaps, dual controls and full blind-flying instrumentation.

In 1937 the type was developed to meet Air Ministry Specification T.40/36 for a monoplane elementary trainer, marking a departure from the standard biplane trainer of which the Tiger Moth was the most familiar but recognising the transition to monoplanes for all new combat aircraft. Compared to the Hawk, the Magister had slightly larger cockpit openings to cope with military Sidcot suits, slightly less span, anti-spin strakes on the rear fuselage, tailwheel instead of skid, and wide-track undercarriage with wheel spats which replaced the earlier trousered effect, although most were operated with bare legs. Fully aerobatic and with a blind flying hood over the rear cockpit, the wooden trainer had a useful turn of speed.

The prototype M.14 Magister/Hawk Trainer III was suitably christened by Mrs F.G. "Blossom" Miles immediately before being given its first test flight by its designer, F. G. Miles. The 800 factory staff showed their appreciation for priorities when they "promptly dealt faithfully with eight barrels of beer in celebration of an exciting job well launched", according to a contemporary report.

First deliveries of the Magister (Latin for master or teacher) went to the Central Flying School in October 1937, and by the time production stopped in January 1941, 1293 had been made, plus another 100 built under licence in Turkey.

It was reportedly ideal for the purpose and pleasant to fly, with a couple of quirks which included reluctance to be coaxed out of a spin. The RAF's first test flight at Martlesham Heath, in fact, resulted in the pilot arriving home without his Magister. The cause was found to be the larger cockpit openings disturbing the airflow, and while raising the tailplane and adding anti-spin strakes cured that problem, the blanking-out of elevator in a sideslip, common to many aircraft from fighters to today's humble Cessna 172, never went away.

The RAF retired its last Magisters in 1948, and as surplus Hawk Trainer Mk IIIs they were used in large numbers by civil flying schools and aero clubs in Britain, with a few finding their way to New Zealand to join the surviving examples of prewar aero club Hawks and Magisters. But in 1957 came a near-fatal blow to British general aviation, which had long relied on sophisticated wooden aeroplanes which were light, clean, pleasant and efficient with their strong wings with lightweight built-up main spars.

Glue technology of the 1930s meant adhesives were less resistant to the effects of mould and fungus than today's epoxies, and marked deterioration of some wartime airframes in the 1950s led to the infamous September 1957 Notice No. 50 from the Air Registration Board. Before the Certificates of Airworthiness of such aircraft could be renewed, it said, "exceptional measures must be taken to dismantle and open up such aircraft and ensure all timber and glued joints have been made good".

The Notice was later amended to become more practical and comprehensive, but it spelled the end of some 140 Magisters still flying at the time. Miles aircraft were particularly susceptible to glue failures because their structures were not protected by varnish, and almost all were scrapped or burnt on the airfields where they last flew. Some survived, however, with three currently airworthy and several more on display in museums.

• Miles M.14A Magister		
Manufacturer:	........Phillips & Powis Aircraft Ltd	
Type:	......................Two-seat primary trainer	
Engine:	....................One de Havilland Gipsy Major 1 4-cylinder inverted, air cooled, 130 hp	
Wingspan:	..............33 ft 10 in	..............10.3 m
Length:	...................24 ft 7½ in	..............7.5 m
Height:	..................6 ft 8 in	...................2 m
Empty weight:	........1286 lb	...................583 kg
Max loaded:	..........1900 lb	...................862 kg
Max range:	............380 miles	...................612 km
Max speed:	...........132 mph	.................212 km/h
First flight:	1937	
In production:	1937-1941	

All three Magisters which survive in flying condition are based in England. They are seen near the Shuttleworth Collection's airfield at Old Warden when the three got together for the first time. P6382 carries the civil registration G-AJRS and is owned by the Shuttleworth Collection. It is painted in the markings of 16 EFTS. T9738/G-AKAT is owned by J.D. Haslam at Breighton, Yorkshire. V1075/G-AKPF was rebuilt by Adrian Brooke and is currently based at the picturesque airfield at Sandown on the Isle of Wight off the south coast of England. *Gordon Bain*

Nanchang CJ-6A

The cockpit is pure military trainer, with Chinese characters to confuse Westerners. *John King*

Present and former Communist countries have a different philosophy when it comes to their machinery. Not for them the emphasis on style and marketing appeal, with its frills and trappings of luxury found in the West; instead they prefer utility and ease of maintenance in usually harsh climates.

Their aircraft, both civil and military, reflect the same principles. Often unremarkable to look at, with paintwork covering the surfaces rather than acting as a sales catcher, they nevertheless have a functionality which appeals to the pilot. And sporting aircraft with Eastern Bloc origins, some of them developed for the military, are proving popular in Western countries.

Chinese aircraft have always been something of a mystery in the West, but one type now becoming available in some numbers shows there is much to commend Eastern design and manufacturing techniques. The State Aircraft Factories are found in several cities, the oldest being the Shenyang works where the Manchu Aeroplane Manufacturing Company was set up by the Japanese invaders of Manchukuo in 1938. When mainland China was combined under the People's Republic of China in 1949 the Manchurian factories were re-established and re-equipped with the help of the Soviet Union, and

through the 1950s aircraft and engine production was a variety of Soviet designs made under licence.

The first of those was the Yak-18, under a licence agreement signed in November 1952. The Soviet two-seat trainer first flew in 1946 and was powered by a 300 hp Ivchenko AI-14RF radial engine. It had prewar origins in the open-cockpit Ya-10 with 120 hp Renault engine, but retractable tailwheel undercarriage and a canopy covering the two seats in tandem brought it into the postwar era. As the CJ-5 the Chinese version differed little from the Yak-18A, but the next model was an indigenous design and the first to enter large-scale production.

The 1960 Chuji Jiaolianji-6 (basic training aircraft 6), or Chujiao-6 or CJ-6, was given a tricycle undercarriage, more in keeping with modern aircraft which pilots of the People's Liberation Army Air Force would progress on to. Power came from a Huosai-6 radial engine of 260 hp, a Chinese version of the Ivchenko, but 285 hp from the Huosai-6A resulted in the CJ-6A with marginally increased cruise speed but a better rate of climb and improved aerobatics capability.

Although the CJ-6 shows obvious signs of shared Yak-18 parentage with the current Yak-52 from Romania, it also has many differences. The wing is three feet longer with dihedral on the outer panels, and the mainwheels retract inwards to lie flush with the bottom skin although the rearward-retracting nosewheel protrudes slightly from the lower fuselage. Tail surfaces are square, and the lack of protuberances and use of flush riveting give a smoothness of outline not seen on many aircraft of similar function. Radial shutters in front of the engine, instead of the cowl flaps found on Western designs, allow faster warmup in winter.

The same philosophy applies to the systems. Batteries lose much of their power in cold conditions, so pneumatics are used for almost everything in the CJ-6A – engine starting, undercarriage lowering and

Nanchang CJ-6A		
Manufacturer:	State Aircraft Factory	
Type:	Two-seat primary trainer	
Engine:	One Huosai-6A 9-cylinder radial, air cooled, 285 hp	
Wingspan:	33 ft 6½ in	10.22 m
Length:	27 ft 9½ in	8.46 m
Height:	10 ft 8 in	3.25 m
Empty weight:	2415 lb	1095 kg
Max loaded:	3088 lb	1400 kg
Max range:	399 miles	640 km
Max speed:	185 mph	297 km/h
First flight:	1960	

retracting, flaps and wheel brakes, with an emergency air system for all but starting. Lack of toe brakes, with brakes applied by a hand lever on the control stick according to which rudder pedal is applied at the time, takes some getting used to for smooth taxying. The large flaps are either up or down, and little painted pegs in the wings and nose relay information to the pilots about where wheels and flaps are.

Control response is such that the CJ-6A just asks to be flown around the sky in aerobatics, which is why this Chinese basic military trainer is finding its way into the West in increasing numbers. Compared to the Yak-52 it's slower in the roll with its longer wings, but the lower power produces the same speed on less fuel, with the added bonus of longer range.

But it can't be compared to Western aircraft, simply because there's no real equivalent. The Yak-52 and Nanchang CJ-6A are in a class all their own.

The Nanchang CJ-6A is notably smooth of outline. Dick Veale flies a New Zealand example near its base at Ardmore, south of Auckland. *John King*

NORTH AMERICAN AT-6 HARVARD/TEXAN

Gordon Bain

Arguably the most important trainer, at least in the Western World in terms of length of service and number of pilots trained, is the Harvard or Texan from the North American stable. More than 17,000 were built in several countries and the AT-6 was in continuous use for almost 60 years, from the late prewar period until the mid-1990s, when the South African Air Force was the last to retire its fleet and set a record for the longest service life of any military aircraft.

North American Aviation grew out of a series of company mergers in the early 1930s and was consolidated at the end of 1934 under James "Dutch" Kindelberger and John Attwood, both ex-Douglas engineers. The company's first project was in pursuit of a USAAC contract for a primary trainer with the intention of establishing its name, and as such it was a success. For many years the company's products set the standard, first among trainers and followed by piston engined fighters and bombers, continuing the tradition well into postwar years with the F-86 Sabre jet fighter.

The NA-16 won the trainer contract and was developed over the next few years with a variety of engines from the 400 hp Wright R-975 and 450 hp

Pratt & Whitney R-985 to the P&W R-1340 Wasp of 500 or 600 hp. The NA-36, which went into production in 1938 with its retractable undercarriage and later metal-covered rear fuselage, became the standard advanced trainer of the Allied forces. Big and powerful, it had all the hydraulic and electrical systems of the most up-to-date fighter of the time, and its flight characteristics were such that any pupil who could master the AT-6 was ready to progress to bigger and faster aircraft.

Further development in Australia resulted in the Commonwealth Aircraft Corporation Wirraway, powered by a geared version of the P&W R-1340. It still had fabric-covered rear fuselage but sported two synchronised forward-facing machine guns as well as a swivelling unit in the rear cockpit, plus hard points under the wings for carrying small bombs. The US Navy used the Texan as the SNJ (Scout Trainer North American) and the British called it the Harvard, in RAF service from 1938. C.G. Grey, editor of *The Aeroplane*, later suggested that if it had the range to fly over Berlin, he was sure all it would take to obtain a Nazi surrender would be the use of fine pitch and maximum revs of its ungeared engine, and the noise would do the rest.

No aircraft, no matter how worthy, remains in military service for ever, but retirement of the AT-6 from the world's air forces has seen only a slight change in emphasis. As one of the more accessible warbirds it sees much pleasure use, particularly for aerobatics, and it is widely used for converting pilots on to bigger things. Most of the younger generation of pilots have not learned on tailwheel types, and the Harvard/Texan's complexity of systems, plus its need for precise control and intolerance of sloppy flying, keeps it in demand as an advanced civil trainer for pilots moving up into the warbirds.

And AT-6s, usually painted these days in bright colours, are still popular with the public at aviation events. They have a special class of their own at the

• North American AT-6 Harvard/Texan		
Manufacturer:	........North American Aviation Inc.	
Type:	.....................Two-seat advanced trainer	
Engine:	...................One Pratt & Whitney R-1340-AN-1 Wasp 9-cylinder radial, air cooled, 550 hp	
Wingspan:	........42 ft ¼ in	...............12.81 m
Length:	...................29 ft	...............8.84 m
Height:	...................11 ft 8½ in	..............3.57 m
Empty weight:	........4271 lb	....................1937 kg
Max loaded:	..........5617 lb	....................2548 kg
Max range:	............870 miles	...............1400 km
Max speed:	............212 mph at 5000 ft	...........341 km/h
First flight:	.............April 1935	
In production:	1936-1954	

Reno air races, and the sight (and sound!) of a sky-darkening mass flypast of Texans at Oshkosh is sure to attract attention. The Roaring Forties is a group of New Zealanders, a few of whom trained on Harvards in their early military careers. They comprise a world-class team specialising in formation aerobatics, carrying on a tradition started by the RNZAF Red Checkers team which entertained crowds with its Harvards a generation ago.

In all countries of the world where there are active warbirds, the AT-6 is sure to be found. In many cases it has been the foundation of the local warbirds movement, big, robust, noisy and spectacular, as well as teaching newcomers what warbirds flying is all about.

Eddie Van Fossen is six times winner of the T-6 races at Reno in this example, trailed here by Ron Hevle.
Philip Makanna

PERCIVAL P.40 PRENTICE

John King

Edgar Percival's company was famous in England during the 1930s for its range of light aircraft, all made of wood and fabric and offering good performance. They were prominent in air racing and several were used for breaking long-distance speed records, including Jean Batten's Gull 6 which she flew solo from England to Brazil in 1935 and England to New Zealand the following year. Alex Henshaw capped off the decade in his Mew Gull by more than halving the England-Cape Town-England return record in February 1939, and Percival Aircraft continued its four-seat line with a development of the Vega Gull, which the RAF called the Proctor, as a communications and radio training aircraft during World War 2.

Towards the end of the war the RAF wanted a primary trainer to replace the venerable Tiger Moth, but with some major differences. Fully enclosed, it was to have room for a third seat in the cabin so that a second trainee might learn something by watching and listening to instructor and pupil. The idea soon fell out of favour with the military but today is regaining acceptance in civil flying training, with four-seaters becoming popular for *ab initio* work.

The P.40 Prentice was Percival's first military design and its first all-metal project. Although it retained a fixed tailwheel undercarriage it did come equipped with comprehensive instrumentation for all-weather work and pneumatic brakes and flaps, while its 250 hp de Havilland Gipsy Queen had a variable pitch propeller. Production totalling more than 350 was undertaken by Percival and Blackburn, as well as Hindustan Aircraft for the Royal Indian Air Force, and others were exported to Argentina and Lebanon.

But it was not one of Percival's more sparkling successes. Larger than the AT-6 Harvard/Texan, the Prentice weighed almost as much but had less than half the power and was noted for being heavy and ponderous. Some of its pilots liked it for its stability as an instrument platform, but that came only after development to correct some unpleasant flying characteristics, including poor spin recovery and a tendency to snap inverted in an unbalanced turn. Upturned wingtips cured the latter problem and larger rudder and elevator area, plus anti-spin strakes on the upper rear fuselage, did something about the spinning, but recovery always needed skill and could be a breathtaking experience as the spin flattened after three turns.

Despite the weight of its controls, the Prentice saw regular aerobatics by the RAF, even if some of its pilots were less than complimentary about its handling. Squadron Leader Stan Greenhow of No 3 FTS Feltwell is reported as saying it was very underpowered and that "aerobatics were awful. It looped OK, but for trainee pilots, slow and barrel rolls were only just possible and tended to be a bit disastrous. It flew like an airborne caravan."

The general opinion was that the Prentice did nothing to enhance Percival Aircraft's reputation as a manufacturer, but the company went on to make other, more successful, military trainers, particularly the P.56 Provost and P.84 Jet Provost.

Retired from RAF service, the surviving 252 Prentices were bought at scrap prices by Freddie Laker and ferried from all corners of the UK to Southend and Stansted for conversion to civil status. Cleared to carry several passengers in the cavernous rear compartment and with extra fuel tanks in the wings, they were expected to appeal to private owners wanting comfortable long-distance touring aircraft. But the venture collapsed, probably because of the suddenly relaxed import controls and ready availability in Britain of smaller Piper and Cessna aircraft, not to mention the thirst, in both fuel and oil, of the Prentice's 250 hp Gipsy Queen engine.

Today Percival's first military design is one of the rarest of warbirds, with only two or three airworthy in the world. It may look as though it was designed by a bureaucratic committee, but it was also the RAF's first primary trainer with an enclosed cockpit and should be remembered as a trend-setter.

New Zealand's only Prentice, flown here above Lake Wanaka by Jay Peters, was originally imported by a religious group for carrying novitiates around Canterbury in its large rear cabin. *John King*

• Percival P.40 Prentice	
Manufacturer:	Percival Aircraft Ltd
Type:	Three-seat primary trainer
Engine:	One de Havilland Gipsy Queen 30-2 6-cylinder inverted, air cooled, 250 hp
Wingspan:	46 ft .... 14.02 m
Length:	31 ft 6 in .... 9.6 m
Height:	8 ft .... 2.44 m
Empty weight:	3250 lb .... 1474 kg
Max loaded:	4350 lb .... 1973 kg
Max range:	300 miles .... 483 km
Max speed:	136 mph .... 219 km/h
First flight:	March 1946

RYAN STM/PT-22

George Bullman's highly polished PT-22 is seen near Monterey, California, during 1994 and shows the differences between the later USAAC trainer and its STM predecessor (opposite). *Gordon Bain*

The original Ryan aircraft manufacturing company was formed in 1922 as Ryan Airlines, later the Mahoney-Ryan Aircraft Corporation, in St Louis, Missouri. Its most famous product was the modified M-1 mailplane, the NYP *Spirit of St Louis* which Charles Lindbergh flew from New York to Paris in 1927 and was later produced as the Brougham. Around that time T. Claude Ryan severed his connections with the company, which merged in 1929 with many others to form the Detroit Aircraft Corporation but collapsed in 1931.

Ryan had kept his Ryan School of Aeronautics going in the meantime, and formed his Ryan Aeronautical Company in 1934. Its first product was the ST, a small sporting trainer of exceptionally clean line, seating two in open cockpits in an all-metal fuselage, with the fabric-covered low wings and their spruce spars braced by external wires. The wheels were faired in and power came from a 95 hp Menasco B-4 inverted in-line engine to give a top speed of almost 140 mph, with handling to match.

That caused a minor sensation although only five were built, but the STA came less than a year later. With its 125 hp Menasco C-4 engine it won races and set a number of light-plane point-to-point and height records, often at the hands of factory pilot

Tex Rankin who also won the 1937 International Aerobatic Championship in a Ryan STA.

The STA Special came next with a supercharged C-4S delivering another 25 hp, and led directly to the STM (Sport Trainer Military) with the same engine, slightly developed with wider cockpit openings as a trainer or "light fighter", as the factory described it, for the Latin American market. A standard STA was entered in USAAC trials in early 1939 at Wright Field and did so well that 15 were ordered as evaluation Y1PT-16s. Others followed as STK (Kinner of similar power) and STW (160 hp Warner Scarab), evolving into the PT-20 series.

Still with Kinner power came the ST-3, looking just the same except when compared side-by-side. Longer, with wider fuselage carrying the circular section of the radial engine, the new Ryan also had a different undercarriage and rudder although the wings remained the same. In the cockpits the equipment was definitely military, and 100 each of the PT-21 and NR-1 were made, followed by more than 1000 of the definitive PT-22 series with 160 hp Kinner R-55, by far the most common variant still flown today as active warbirds.

The largest export market was not Latin America but the Netherlands East Indies, now Indonesia. The Dutch colony had an active navy and air force, but when war broke out in Europe in 1939 they had to find a new way to train pilots, all previous training and qualifying having been done in the Netherlands. Tiger Moths were hired from the Surabaya Flying Club before orders were filled from late 1940 for 84 STM-2 landplane and 24 STM-S2 floatplane trainers with 36 sets of floats.

The Ryans were busy as primary, basic and advanced trainers all rolled into one, as well as aerobatics, blind flying and everything except bombing and gunnery training.

After the Japanese over-ran Java, 34 of the surviving STMs were evacuated by ship to Australia and used by the RAAF, but several were captured and

• Ryan STM	
Manufacturer:	Ryan Aeronautical Company
Type:	Two-seat primary trainer
Engine:	One Menasco C-4S Pirate 4-cylinder inverted supercharged, air cooled, 150 hp
Wingspan:	29 ft 11 in ....9.12 m
Length:	22 ft 8½ in ....6.92 m
Height:	6 ft 11 in ....2.11 m
Empty weight:	1058 lb ....480 kg
Max loaded:	1700 lb ....771 kg
Max range:	375 miles ....604 km
Max speed:	160 mph ....258 km/h
First flight:	8 June 1934
In production:	1935-1942

flown by the invaders. Lt H.F.C. Holts, a Dutch officer who was captured but later escaped, wrote of his experiences in a Ryan company newsletter in 1943. "During this officer's imprisonment near Batavia Air Field he saw the Japs using the Netherlands East Indies fleet of Ryan landplanes regularly for aerobatic training and formation flying. The one enjoyable sight he saw during his captivity was when two of the planes collided in midair as the result of poor piloting."

New Zealand Warbirds Association president Trevor Bland flies one of the surviving Netherlands East Indies Ryan STMs in December 1998, its first time airborne for more than 40 years. S-53 was imported into New Zealand in the 1950s and flew for some time as ZK-BEM. In a derelict state it was presented to Auckland's Museum of Transport & Technology in 1967 on the condition that it be restored to flying condition. An historic agreement between MOTAT and the Warbirds Association has seen it rebuilt by a Warbirds group, complete with its original wartime colour scheme and supercharged 150 hp Menasco Pirate engine. *John King*

YAKOVLEV YAK-52

These two Yak-52s, flown by Bill Rolfe (left) and Sir Kenneth Hayr near Auckland, New Zealand, are of recent production in Romania. *John King*

A warbird is usually defined as an ex-military aircraft which is no longer in production and has been retired into private, civil use. Within these pages are some exceptions in the form of elderly aircraft still operated by air forces – plus another anomaly, a military trainer still in production but finding its way into the hands of the private, more sporting pilot.

The collapse of the Iron Curtain and the availability of previously unaccepted Eastern Bloc aircraft in the Western world has had a marked effect on the variety of types regularly seen flying. The Russian Yak-52 and its close cousin the Nanchang from China are just two examples which offer lower operating costs than the older Western equivalent, the T-6 Harvard advanced trainer. Their general sportiness appeals to private pilots who want good handling qualities and aerobatic capabilities, usually at a level below serious competition. Indeed, pilots praise its handling characteristics and report that there is no current Western equivalent.

The Yak-52's origins date from prewar days with the 1937 Ya-10, an open-cockpit two-seat trainer powered by a 120 hp Renault. Originally known as the

AIR-10 after A.I. Rykov, a high-ranking Communist leader, it was renamed for its designer, Aleksandir Sergeivich Yakovlev, after Rykov fell a victim to one of Stalin's periodic purges. The Ya-10 was later developed into the Yak-18, still a trainer but with its tandem cockpits enclosed and sporting a retractable undercarriage.

A single-seat competition development, the Yak-18PS, was redesigned into the Yak-50 in time for the 1976 World Aerobatic Championships at Kiev. The former Communist countries were noted for their serious entries into competition flying, and the Soviet team took most of the places and the team prize at Kiev with their Yak-50s, which came from the drawing boards of Sergei Yakovlev, son of Aleksandir, and Yuri Yankievich.

Of all-metal construction with semi-monocoque fuselage, the new single-seater was given a 1.2 metre reduction in span by deleting the centre section, and all dihedral came from the wing taper with a straight top-surface. The Yak-52, using the same Vedeneev M-14P radial engine but less nimble than its single-seat competition stablemate by virtue of its extra weight and length, was announced in 1978 as a replacement for the Yak-18 series which had been in service for more than 30 years. Design work proceeded rapidly and production was undertaken in Bacau, eastern Romania, where the type is still made, although factory remanufactured examples are also available, some of them from Lithuania.

Wing construction is simplified by having the stalky tricycle undercarriage only semi-retract to sit proud of the structure, affecting mainly cruise speed. It has the secondary advantage of protecting the structure should the pilot neglect to lower things before landing. For such occasions the factory thoughtfully provides a line on the two propeller blades, to enable further and more accurate deliberate trimming of the inevitably shortened wooden paddle units and allow the aircraft to be carefully ferried back to base in an

• Yakovlev Yak-52	
Manufacturer:	Intreprinderea de Avioane Bacau
Type:	Two-seat primary trainer
Engine:	One Vedeneev M-14P 9-cylinder radial, air cooled, 360 hp
Wingspan:	30 ft 6¼ in .... 9.30 m
Length:	25 ft 5 in .... 7.745 m
Height:	8 ft 10¼ in .... 2.70 m
Empty weight:	2205 lb .... 1000 kg
Max loaded:	2844 lb .... 1290 kg
Max range:	341 miles .... 550 km
Max speed:	186 mph .... 300 km/h at 500 m
First flight:	1979
In production:	1979-present

emergency. The nine-cylinder supercharged 360 hp M-14P is normally hidden behind shutters, typical of Russian and other eastern European aircraft, and starting is by compressed air from an on-board bottle, Siberian winters not being kind to aircraft batteries.

The Yak-52's military origins are highlighted by the tachometer which reads in percentage of rpm. Ninety-nine percent for takeoff can be held for five minutes, 90 percent for 10 minutes and maximum continuous is 82 percent, at which setting all aerobatics are flown. Instruments are labelled mostly in Cyrillic script and read in kilometres per hour, which appeals to modern-day sporting pilots because it makes everything seem like jet speeds.

This modern classic's availability in the West is generally considered to be one of the better things to happen in aviation in recent years, and Yak-52 pilots tend to be a cheerful lot.

Garth Hogan of the KGB and Paul Hughan are half a Yak-52 formation display team based at Auckland's North Shore Airfield, New Zealand. John King

ANTONOV AN-2

All radial engines puff smoke on starting, and the Shvetsov ASh-62M does it just as well as any other. This An-2 is now part of Gerald Rhodes's growing collection here at Wanaka, New Zealand. *John King*

Antonov's ubiquitous transport biplane is a beast of superlatives. Not only is it the largest single-engine biplane to have been made in any quantity, but that quantity is also higher than any other. More than 5000 were built in the USSR for the Soviet armed forces, Aeroflot and other civilian organisations before production stopped in the mid-1960s, but that wasn't the end of it. Well over 1000 have been made in China as the Shijiazhuang Y-5 and production continued at the WSK-PZL Mielec factory where more than 10,000 have been turned out. Only the Beechcraft Bonanza, which dates from 1947, has had a longer production record.

Given the code name Colt by some United Nations analyst with a sense of humour, the An-2 has served in a variety of roles exceeded only by production numbers themselves. As well as the military paratrooper version with six tip-up seats along each side of the cabin, the standard passenger An-2 carries 12 people who are less likely to depart in flight, or up to 1500 kg of cargo. The executive model has seats for five, with foldaway tables in between, while six patients and their medical attendants can be carried in the ambulance version. An-2s have been fitted with floats or made for geophysical survey, high-altitude meteorological research, photogrammetry or television relay, but the most common model is for agricultural use, fitted with a 1400 litre hopper for liquids or dry chemicals.

As might be expected with an aeroplane built in such numbers, the An-2 has served in many countries outside the manufacturing three. With the exception of France, the Netherlands, Egypt and Sudan, all the nations operating An-2s have been members of the Communist Bloc where the Colt has been the standard general-purpose aircraft.

With the collapse of the Iron Curtain and the need for those countries to export their products and make their way in a commercial world, some of the previously unavailable aircraft are finding ready markets in the West. Notable among them are the Yak-52 and Nanchang CJ-6A, but the sheer novelty value of a massive single-engine biplane, anachronistic, far from elegant and unlike anything ever produced in Western nations, is seeing them trickle into other parts of Europe. Accounts of delivery flights invariably describe the bureaucracy still prevailing in Eastern Europe and wax eloquent about the quality and especially the strength of the local vodka, but liberating an An-2 to England is child's play compared to the drama of flying one to the other side of the world.

Neville Cameron, of Coromandel east of Auckland, New Zealand, has imported a number of Yak-52s, and his eye was caught by a semi-derelict An-2 at the Lithuanian State Aviation Factory. Being blessed with a disposition not content with sitting in front of television, he dreamed of the trip of a lifetime, flying an aeroplane from Europe home to New Zealand. It was an experience, all right – not one to be repeated but nothing less than memorable.

The flight was in two stages, with a long pause at Oman with technical problems and to avoid the monsoon season further east. Cost was a major factor. Avgas is becoming increasingly rare and expensive, up to $US2.00 a litre, especially in those parts of the world where the raw product is pumped from beneath the ground, and oil of a variety to satisfy a thirsty 1000 hp radial engine is even more scarce.

But with the help of a Lithuanian instructor and several New Zealand pilot friends, Cameron brought his An-2 home. He has some words of advice for anyone contemplating a similar expedition: "If you do not have an autopilot, limit legs to six hours absolute; attempt to spend a day resting between legs; don't drink the water; spend some time previously on a small task with your future companions; do not fly with someone who has just given up smoking; a designated trouble shooter is desirable; and rural Australians are the nicest people in the world."

After flying this An-2 half-way around the world from Lithuania to New Zealand, Neville Cameron finds cruising along the Coromandel Peninsula near his home to be a piece of cake. *John King*

• Antonov An-2 Colt		
Origin:	Antonov Design Bureau	
Type:	Biplane transport	
Engine:	One Shvetsov ASh-62M 9-cylinder radial, air cooled, 1000 hp	
Wingspan:	59 ft 8 in (upper)	18.18 m
Length:	41 ft 10 in	12.47 m
Height:	13 ft 1½ in	4.0 m
Empty weight:	7605 lb	3450 kg
Max loaded:	12,125 lb	5500 kg
Max range:	485 miles	900 km
Max speed:	160 mph	258 km/h
Cruise speed:	115 mph	185 km/h
First flight:	31 August 1947	
In production:	1948-1985	

AUSTER

Keith McLean and Alastair Chaffey fly their Auster V over the Rakaia River. One of 790 Mk Vs built, TJ342 was flown from 1944 by No 665 Canadian Squadron in Holland and Germany before going to No 83 Communications Group. It was imported into New Zealand in 1950 and has spent most of its years not far from this spot in the South Island. *John King*

In developing a new category of aircraft early in World War 2, the military authorities in both Britain and the United States effectively reinvented the wheel, going back to military aviation's roots but giving fresh thought to an old problem.

The very first use of aircraft in warfare had been as artillery spotters, originally balloons, and World War 1 brought more development. Balloons were still used, but the aeroplane, with its ability to change height and position much more quickly, came into favour for artillery spotting. Two-seaters were used, with the gunnery officer in the back doing the observing while the pilot got on with the flying. Single-seater scouts were developed to intercept the observation aircraft, and so the whole business of military aviation developed.

Two-seaters were equipped with a defensive machine gun for the observer, and the concept lasted all through the 1920s and 1930s, with army cooperation aircraft growing bigger and faster to keep pace with the fighters on which they were based. As they increased in weight and landing speed so their need for larger airfields grew, but in 1939 a much lighter

aeroplane, still a two-seater but unarmed, was flown by the RAF and Royal Artillery Flying Club to test its suitability as an AOP (air observation post) for artillery spotting duties. A small aircraft could use unprepared airstrips near the mobile gun sites, and a number of artillery officers were private pilots. It was easier to train such officers in the necessary flying techniques rather than teach air force pilots the specialised craft of observing and correcting artillery fire.

They used a re-engined Taylorcraft Plus C, made under licence as a local development of the American Taylorcraft (the Taylor brothers were originally English and their original Cub was later developed as the Piper Cub). Powered by 90 hp Cirrus Minor in place of the original 55 hp Lycoming O-145, the Plus D had good performance and, with suitable modifications, was deemed suitable for the task.

One hundred were initially ordered, but the Ministry of Aircraft Production wanted them given a generic name, in line with standard British military procedure. Icarus was eliminated because of structural failure on its initial test flight, but the trend towards strong winds such as Hurricane, Tempest and Typhoon brought the suggestion of Auster, the Latin name for a warm southerly breeze.

Hundreds of Austers were used in all Allied theatres from 1942. Unarmed and completely defenceless against attacking enemy fighters, they actually suffered more from shells fired by their own side, only six of the 37 operational casualties suffered by AOP squadrons in Europe being directly attributed to enemy aircraft. All Auster pilots had to be adept at low flying to take advantage of the cover of houses, villages and natural landscape features, and the necessity to fly everywhere at below 50 feet was a popular part of their training.

By war's end the Auster had sprouted flaps, tailwheel and 130 hp engine in the form of Gipsy Major (Mk III) or Lycoming O-290 (Mk V). Postwar production for the civil market saw Austers in most

• Auster V	
Manufacturer:	Taylorcraft Aeroplanes (England) Ltd
Type:	Air observation post
Engine:	One Lycoming O-290-3 4-cylinder horizontally opposed air cooled, 130 hp
Wingspan:	36 ft .... 10.97 m
Length:	22 ft 5 in .... 6.83 m
Height:	8 ft .... 2.44 m
Empty weight:	1160 lb .... 526 kg
Max loaded:	1900 lb .... 862 kg
Max range:	250 miles .... 402 km
Max speed:	130 mph .... 209 km/h
First flight:	May 1939 (Plus C)

Commonwealth countries, while military versions were made until the helicopter took over the army cooperation role. The last production military Auster was the ungainly AOP.9 with 180 hp Blackburn Cirrus Bombardier engine, and the largest concentration of service Austers is found in England at the Museum of Army Flying, Middle Wallop, Hampshire.

As the MAF's Stephen White says, "Most people do not realise the significance of the Auster. The type served from 1942 to 1967, and for all but one of those years the aircraft were being shot at somewhere in the world!"

Low flying practice over the rural countryside was a popular but necessary activity for artillery spotting officers who flew all the Allied AOPs. This top view of the Auster V shows the generous wing area for which the type was always known. The docile handling and generous power from a 130 hp Lycoming O-290 made it a most useful AOP, seen in all theatres of World War 2. *John King*

BEECH MODEL 18

The Confederate Air Force's C-45 is flown near Midland, Texas. *Philip Makanna*

Only when the final three Beechcraft Super H18s were delivered to Japan Air Lines on 26 November 1969 was production of the Model 18 finally at an end. The first had flown in January 1937 and the continuous production of 32 years set an aviation record at the time, since broken by the Antonov An-2 and Beech's own Model 35 Bonanza which started in 1947 and is still being made.

Beech Aircraft Corporation was started in April 1932 when husband and wife Walter and Olive Beech went out on their own. For a new company, its first product was remarkable – the Beech Model 17 (the previous 16 had been designs in conjunction with other companies) was a fast, comfortable cabin biplane which, with its reverse stagger which put the top wing behind the bottom for aerodynamic and visibility reasons, was instantly recognisable. It was also badly timed, an expensive aircraft for corporate or wealthy private use when the Depression was starting to bite.

The Staggerwing came with a variety of radial engines and a note added, perhaps rashly, to the sales brochure casually mentioned that it was also available with the Wright Cyclone engine. Sanford Mills in Maine took up the challenge and ordered an A17F

with 690 hp engine, which gave the aircraft a cartoon look with its massive radial engine and large trousered fixed undercarriage. Contrary to expectations, Sanford company pilot Bob Fogg successfully handled the Cyclone-powered Beech, with its 215 mph cruise and tricky ground handling, throughout 1934. It was then sold to Howard Hughes but was never heard of after 1937.

Beech Aircraft was only three years old, with the Model 17 in full production, when work started on the next aircraft, the Model 18. Whereas the Staggerwing had wooden biplane wings and a steel tube fuselage, all covered in fabric, the new twin was a cantilever monoplane of all-metal construction. The fuselage and wings were stressed skin construction, with a truss-type centre section of welded chrome steel tubing, heat treated to a strength of 180,000 pounds per square inch.

The first engines were 320 hp Wright R-760-E2 radials, but various models of Pratt & Whitney, Jacobs and Wright engines were offered during the 1930s. The feeder liner, seating six passengers plus two crew, found acceptance in Canada more readily than in its parent country, and by 1939 it was starting to be noticed in military circles.

Examples were delivered to the Philippine Army Air Corps for aerial photography after being selected by the Chief of Staff of the American military mission to the Philippines, one Lt Col Dwight Eisenhower. Beech 18s participated in a USAAC evaluation at Wright Field in 1939, and some were sold to China for pilot training and as M18R light tactical bombers, fitted with gun turrets and bomb racks. A USAAF order for 150 similarly equipped Model 18s followed in 1941.

More than 5000 of a final production total of 7088 were modified Beech 18s supplied to Allied military forces. The USAAF had C-45 transports, AT-7 navigation trainers, AT-11 Kansan bombing and gunnery trainers and F2 photo reconnaissance air-

craft, the US Navy called them JRB Expeditors and SNB Kansans, and the Canadians and British knew them as Expeditors. Beech Model 18s were used for training some 90 per cent of American bombardiers and navigators of World War 2.

Nor were they all retired immediately after the war. The factory refurbished 2263 of them between 1952 and 1961 under a US Government programme and the USAF used a decreasing number of C-45s until November 1963. The US Navy retired its last SNB-5s in July 1972 and the US Army operated five Beech 18s as utility and liaison transports as late as 1976. They continue to fly in private hands, ex-military Model 18s used by various Confederate Air Force wings and other warbirds groups as appropriate transport for their members.

Mike MacIntyre of Redwood Estates, California, bought this Beech 18 in Canada late in 1997. Painted in RCAF markings, it was photographed during May 1998. *Gordon Bain*

• Beech D18S	
Manufacturer:	Beech Aircraft Corporation
Type:	Light transport/trainer
Engines:	Two Pratt & Whitney R-985-AN-14B Wasp Junior 9-cylinder radial, air cooled, 450 hp
Wingspan:	47 ft 7 in ....14.5 m
Length:	33 ft 11½ in ....10.35 m
Height:	9 ft 2½ in ....2.8 m
Empty weight:	5635 lb ....2558 kg
Max loaded:	8750 lb ....3980 kg
Max range:	1200 miles ....1931 km
Max speed:	225 mph ....362 km/h
First flight:	15 January 1937
In production:	1937-1969

CESSNA L-19/O-1 BIRD DOG

Generous flap and wing area give the Bird Dog a slow approach speed and guaranteed short landing roll. *John King*

A general rule in aviation is that as anything is developed it gains weight and complexity, despite any intention for it to retain its original role. Usually that is a result of the never-ending quest for more power for either more performance or greater load-carrying capability, or one at the expense of the other, but occasionally the role undergoes a subtle change and takes the aircraft with it.

Air observation posts (AOPs) started out at the beginning of World War 2 with American Grasshoppers (militarised Piper J-3 Cubs and similar minimal products from other manufacturers) and British Austers (local derivatives of the American Taylorcraft). They were ideal for flitting around at low level near friendly artillery sites, popping up for their artillery officer pilots to observe the fall of shells, and with their light weight they could operate out of unlikely looking patches of ground nearby.

The next development in the liaison series was the Stinson L-5 Sentinel, with three times the L-4's power but still carrying a crew of two, or pilot and stretcher patient in the case of the L-5B. At first sharing the war duties, from 1945 L-5s took over from the Grasshoppers, which became extinct, while the British developed their Auster into muscular aircraft with ever-increasing weight – until the helicopter came along and killed those off, too.

In 1949 the Americans saw a need for an all-metal liaison and observation aircraft, and Cessna came up with its Model 305A. Sharing the landing gear, wings and tail with the existing Cessna 170, it had a six-cylinder Continental engine and a new fuselage which, narrowing from the wing roots at the top, offered a good downwards view for its two occupants seated in tandem. The following year Cessna won the US Army competition and a contract was signed for deliveries as the L-19A. Further orders followed until a total of 3431 Bird Dogs left the Cessna factory, for US Army and Marine Corps use as well as exports to more than a dozen countries, in several variants which included dual controls and extra radio and navigation equipment.

The Bird Dog saw action in Korea, where it served the type's usual useful purpose, but its role started to undergo a subtle change. Artillery spotting was still important, but during the latter stages of World War 2 some AOPs had been used as marker aircraft for air strikes. By the time of the war in Vietnam from about 1960 the Bird Dogs were assuming the role of forward air control (FAC) aircraft, marking targets with smoke rockets and generally keeping an aerial eye on ground movements. Other tasks, equally valuable, included clearing a base perimeter in the morning, in case of overnight Vietcong infiltration, or scouting ahead of a road convoy, searching for likely ambush spots.

Other aircraft later took over the dangerous FAC duties in Vietnam and its neighbouring countries which were inevitably drawn into the fighting. The L-19, renamed O-1 in 1962, was largely replaced by the O-2, a military version of the Cessna 337 in-line twin with its engines fore and aft, while the most popular with its pilots was the OV-10 Bronco, much bigger, heavier and faster with two turboprop engines and plenty of stores under the wings.

Any warbird which offers the economy of a light aircraft is going to be popular with private owners, and the Cessna Bird Dog has found a ready place among enthusiasts in many countries. Its handling qualities are typically Cessna, but it will spin if provoked, and the maximum flap setting of 60 degrees (not permitted in the US Army manual) allows a very steep descent and short landing roll. Opening windows front and back give excellent vision and ventilation, although not all countries share the tropical temperatures of Vietnam. Its speed with just over 200 hp and a fixed pitch propeller may not be shattering, but a restored O-1 with the bullet holes patched is a fun aeroplane.

Both Ross Ewing (front) and John Denton flew FAC duties in Vietnam during their RNZAF careers, although not in Bird Dogs. This O-1A is based at Ardmore, Auckland. *John King*

• Cessna L-19/O-1 Bird Dog	
Manufacturer:	Cessna Aircraft Company
Type:	Light observation/liaison aircraft
Engine:	One Continental O-470-11 6-cylinder horizontally opposed, air cooled, 213 hp
Wingspan:	36 ft ... 10.97 m
Length:	25 ft 9½ in ... 7.86 m
Height:	7 ft 3½ in ... 2.22 m
Empty weight:	1614 lb ... 732 kg
Max loaded:	2400 lb ... 1089 kg
Max range:	530 miles ... 853 km
Max speed:	115 mph ... 184 km/h at sea level
First flight:	1950
In production:	1950-1961

CESSNA 180

The markings are starting to fade now, more than 20 years after this Cessna 180 was retired from military service. *John King*

When the Australian Army wanted a liaison/observation aircraft in 1961 its choices were limited as the Cessna L-19 Bird Dog production run had just finished. The war in Vietnam was hotting up, however, and such an aircraft was an established part of any Western military arm's materiel, so the decision was made to buy a number of Cessna's current four-seat utility model, the 180. Unlike most military aircraft, the type was not given any specific designation and was always known by the Australians as simply the Cessna 180.

Cessna introduced its 180 model in 1953, and produced more than 6000 examples during its 28-year production. A no-nonsense four-seater with tailwheel undercarriage and powered by a 225 hp (later examples had 230 hp) Continental engine, it offered a reasonable cruising speed coupled with an ability to lift good loads in and out of modestly prepared airstrips. Although the Cessna 180 has been out of production for almost 20 years it still appeals to the private owner, particularly in rural areas away from sealed runways.

Carrying a bigger load and offering more operational flexibility than the Bird Dog, the Cessna 180 was highly popular with the Australian pilots. Some two dozen were ordered straight from the Cessna factory, and on arrival in Australia were modified for military use by Hawker de Havilland at Bankstown, Sydney. The major changes from the civilian model included a clear panel in the cabin roof with associated local strengthening, military radios, 24 volt electrical system, photography hatch in the floor and strong points for slinging loads under the wings. The changes added a couple of hundred pounds to the empty weight, but as the 180 usually flew with a crew of two the reduced payload made little difference.

The original batch was delivered to the RAAF which trained artillery officers in their operation, although air observation post duties had always been part of Army pilot training, usually on Bird Dogs in Germany with NATO. The 16th Army Light Aircraft Company was formed in December 1960 and took over that task, and in Vietnam the Cessna 180s were principally used for dawn patrols, reconnaissance and all communications work as well as the AOP role for artillery spotting. They were not used for forward air control as such, although they carried target marker rockets under the wings and could fulfil that function when necessary.

Returned from Vietnam and replaced by 19 Pilatus Turbo Porters in the mid-1970s, the Australian Army Cessna 180s were mostly retired into less hectic civilian use. With their camera hatches they were popular with survey companies and some were operated on forestry patrol for photography and spotting.

A98-063 was registered VH-TVB after some 5000 hours of Army use and had its day-glo orange wingtips repainted yellow for visibility, its overall olive drab paint otherwise blending in well against the background of pine trees on forestry work. From there it went to a pastoral company on Flinders Island, Bass Strait, before being bought in the early 1980s by Max Balfour.

The Cessna 180 still wears its original Army olive drab paint, and the only major change is the installation of a STOL kit as it is used for photography and other commercial work from airstrips in hilly country, based on his farm strip at Mullumbimby, northern New South Wales. Various bullet holes in the tail have been patched, and it still bears traces of holes for an M-60 machine gun mount in the right-hand door sill. The extra empty weight means less payload than a normal example, but the cabin skylights are a useful feature which every Cessna 180 owner believes should have been part of the aircraft from the start.

Most warbirds have been retired into purely recreational and airshow use, but the Australian Army's Cessna 180s are still useful for the sort of commercial work for which the type has long been famous in general aviation.

Max Balfour bases his ex-Australian Army Cessna 180 on his farm at Mullumbimby, northern New South Wales, still painted in its original olive drab but with yellow panels for recognition. *John King*

• Cessna 180		
Manufacturer:	........Cessna Aircraft Company	
Type:	......................Light observation/liaison aircraft	
Engine:	...................One Continental O-470-K 6-cylinder horizontally opposed, air cooled, 230 hp	
Wingspan:	..............35 ft 10 in	...............10.92 m
Length:	...................25 ft 9½ in	..............7.85 m
Height:	...................7 ft 9 in	...................2.36 m
Empty weight:	........1800 lb	...................816 kg
Max loaded:	...........2800 lb	...................1270 kg
Max range:	............950 miles	...............1528 km
Max speed:	............170 mph	.................274 km/h at sea level
First flight:	1952	
In production:	1953-1981	

DE HAVILLAND DH84 DRAGON

The Dragon pilot, in this case Stan Smith, sits all by himself in the sharp end with a magnificent view.
John King

Conceived as a warplane, it made its mark as a civil airliner in prewar days. And yet half the world's four airworthy examples, all of which wear civilian paint schemes, were made as military aircraft during World War 2. The de Havilland Dragon is something of an enigma.

Back in the early 1930s the DH83 Fox Moth, carrying three or four passengers and a pilot on the power of one 130 hp Gipsy Major engine, was an economic success among British charter operators, including Hillman Saloon Coaches and Airways Ltd. Edward Hillman had the idea that a bigger biplane, powered by two Gipsy Majors and carrying six or eight passengers, would be a good idea and dropped by the de Havilland works to have a chat about it.

Chief designer Arthur Hagg just happened to have something on hand, a light bomber he was working on for the Iraqi Air Force. Long before the days of Saddam Hussein and his Scud missiles, when chemical warfare was a matter of intermittent bathing habits and eating plenty of garlic, local tribesmen who got a bit uppity could apparently be subdued by the sight of one of de Havilland's square-rigged biplanes and

the threatening roar of two Gipsy Majors in doubtful synchronisation. Amateur lepidopterist Geoffrey de Havilland's Moth family of light aeroplanes was well established, but no moths ever sported guns or dropped things which went bang, so the new light bomber needed another name. What better for a little fire-breather than a Dragon?

It offered good capacity within its simple plywood box fuselage, and Hillman promptly ordered four off the drawing board, with some modifications. The four 200 pound bombs and various Lewis machine guns, not to mention the navigator/bomb aimer and wireless operator/air gunner, were thought to be superfluous for the average British regional routes, but that left all the more room for paying passengers. By the time production stopped in 1937, 115 DH84 Dragons were flying, most of them with third-level and charter airlines in several countries but also as military DH84Ms for the Iraqi, Danish and Portuguese air forces.

The type was well established among Australian airlines, and 11 were impressed into RAAF service as radio and navigation trainers in September 1939. The RAAF needed more and requested DH89s with their more powerful engines which were better able to cope with higher temperatures, but all British production of the 200 hp Gipsy Six engines was needed for home use in the RAF's DH89B Dominies. Gipsy Majors were in better local supply, being made by General Motors Holden for the Tiger Moth production in both Australia and New Zealand, so all the existing Dragon tooling and jigs, along with those for the DH94 Moth Minor, were packaged up and sent off to Bankstown, Sydney.

The Australians made 87 more Dragons between September 1942 and May 1943. Built exactly according to factory specifications and without the benefit of years of tweaking the rigging to get the best performance, the first examples when test flown had a single-engine height of 2000 feet – below sea level! That was soon sorted out, although the DH84 always was

typically British in that a twin-engine aircraft was just that, and any thoughts of single-engine performance involved paddocks not too far away.

Fifty-three Australian-made Dragons survived the war to be sold to local airlines. Time, mishaps, deterioration of glue joints and timber, plus the ravages of damp and termites, have all meant that elderly wood-and-fabric aeroplanes quietly fade from the active scene, and of the total of 202 DH84s produced in England and Australia just 11 still exist. Four of those are airworthy, another four are being rebuilt to fly and the remainder are static museum exhibits, all reminding today's general public of a more gentle era when a civil airliner could also be a warbird.

To many people, the decade of the 1930s represents the Golden Age of flying, as exemplified by a Dragon in the sunset, flown here by Stan Smith. This Australian-made DH84 was restored to flying in Auckland, New Zealand, in April 1997 after a lengthy rebuild caused by engine failure after takeoff.
John King

• de Havilland DH84 Dragon	
Manufacturer:	The de Havilland Aircraft Company
Type:	Light transport, radio/navigation trainer
Engines:	Two de Havilland Gipsy Major 1 4-cylinder inverted, air cooled, 130 hp
Wingspan:	47 ft 4 in ..... 14.43 m
Length:	34 ft 6 in ..... 10.52 m
Height:	10 ft 1 in ..... 3.07 m
Empty weight:	2385 lb ..... 1082 kg
Max loaded:	4500 lb ..... 2041 kg
Max range:	460 miles ..... 740 km
Max speed:	134 mph ..... 216 km/h
First flight:	24 November 1932
In production:	1932-1937, 1942-1943

DE HAVILLAND DH89 DOMINIE/RAPIDE

A military version of the DH89 was offered in 1935 for coastal patrol, but wartime DH89B production was intended as radio and navigation trainers. Harry Norton patrols the seaward side of Kapiti Island near Wellington, New Zealand, in his Dominie. *John King*

Given the circumstances of the mid-1930s and the British Government's lack of recognition of the re-armament of Germany, it was inevitable that many British manufacturers were almost casually offering military versions of otherwise harmless commercial aircraft.

Typical was the respected firm The de Havilland Aircraft Company, still persevering with wood-and-fabric biplanes when the USA and much of Europe were enjoying the advantages offered by all-metal cantilever monoplanes. True, its plywood DH88 Comet, a specialised racer, proved fastest in the London-Melbourne air race of October 1934, but its crew of two were exhausted at the end. By way of contrast, the pilot and copilot of the equally new KLM DC-2, which carried passengers and mail and finished not far behind them after a forced landing in bad weather, were relaxed and fresh by comparison.

That same race saw the international debut of another de Havilland model, the DH89, with its fabric-covered plywood fuselage closely modelled on that of the DH84 Dragon but with elegantly tapered wings and its fixed undercarriage faired into the engine nacelles. Powered by two of the new 200 hp Gipsy Six engines, it was at first called the Dragon Six, but

that was soon changed to Rapide as it cruised some 20 mph faster than the DH84. A new DH89, crewed by three New Zealanders, finished fifth in the handicap section after a long delay caused by running into a fence in the dark in outback Australia, and was also the first aircraft directly to link England and New Zealand, the most remote British Dominion, when it flew across the Tasman Sea after the race.

Like the Dragon, the Rapide seated a single pilot in the extreme nose with six to eight passengers in the cabin, but the company announced a military version in 1935, intended for coastal reconnaissance or to escort torpedo bombers and shipping. The pilot had a Vickers machine gun mounted in the cockpit beside him, firing forwards out through the right-hand fuselage side and with the feed belts under his seat. At the rear of the cabin was a defensive gun for the wireless operator/gunner and behind the pilot was the bomb aimer's station, sighting through a hole in the floor. The two 100 pound and four 20 pound bombs were stowed internally, dropping through spring-loaded trapdoors in the bottom of the fuselage.

But the DH89 Rapide was best known during the 1930s not as a light bomber but as a feeder airliner, comfortable and possessing a good short-field performance and even being said to be able to maintain height on one engine. Sales were good in many Commonwealth countries and the type was still in production when Britain declared war on Germany in 1939 and suddenly needed many more aircraft.

By then the DH89 had sprouted flaps and a few other refinements to become the DH89A, and wartime production with 200 hp Gipsy Queen engines and military fittings became the DH89B Dominie, Scottish for schoolmaster as the erstwhile airliner was used as a radio and navigation trainer. As the de Havilland works were busy with other projects, especially the Mosquito, DH89B output was mostly by Brush Coachworks, its workers skilled in working with wood. More than 700 DH89s were

made in the 10 years it remained in production.

As well as its training role, the Dominie was used extensively as a communications aircraft. Its seating capacity was ideal for transporting ferry pilots to and from their collection points, and DH89Bs maintained a form of airline service for military personnel. After World War 2 they were retained by a number of air forces for many years and also fitted easily back into the civil world, being active as charter and scheduled third-level airliners well into the 1970s before age and general deterioration of their wooden structure caught up with them.

Dave Gray relived a bit of aviation history by flying this DH89B to 22nd place overall, the only vintage type to qualify in the 1969 London-Sydney Air Race, 35 years after the type first flew in the London-Melbourne event. Here he is seen above the Whangaparaoa Peninsula, north of Auckland. New Zealand civil DH89Bs have kept their wartime Dominie name while other countries have reverted to civil Rapides. *John King*

• de Havilland DH89 Dominie/Rapide		
Manufacturer:	.......The de Havilland Aircraft Company	
Type:	.....................Light transport	
Engines:	...............Two de Havilland Gipsy Queen 2 6-cylinder inverted, air cooled, 200 hp	
Wingspan:	.............48 ft	.........................14.6 m
Length:	.................34 ft 6 in	...................10.52 m
Height:	.................10 ft 3 in	...................3.12 m
Empty weight:	......3230 lb	.....................1465 kg
Max loaded:	..........5500 lb	.....................2497 kg
Max range:	...........520 miles	.................837 km
Max speed:	...........150 mph	...................242 km/h at sea level
First flight:	.............17 April 1934	
In production:	1934-1944	

DE HAVILLAND DH104 DEVON AND DH114 HERON

Four ex-RNZAF Devons are airworthy on the New Zealand civil register. This example, flown here by James Dalziell, is now based at Whangarei. *John King*

Towards the end of World War 2 the de Havilland Aircraft Company saw a postwar market for a light cabin-class twin seating eight to ten passengers. As a feeder liner it would replace the venerable DH89 Rapide series, plus competing but prewar aircraft such as the Avro Anson and Airspeed Courier, and in addition have other air ambulance, survey, executive transport and military applications.

But while it was intended to be a straight Rapide replacement, the new airliner was unlike anything else which had emerged from the factory at Hatfield. Almost the entire range of de Havilland's prewar aircraft featured fabric-covered wood and plywood construction (a method continued for years yet with the balsa/plywood sandwich fuselage of the Vampire and Venom jet fighters), but the DH104 was all-metal. It was also the company's first production aircraft with retractable tricycle undercarriage and had half the usual number of wings, cantilevered instead of strutted and wire-braced. Power came from two supercharged Gipsy Queen engines producing much more than the DH89's 200 hp each, but although the speed was rather higher its empty weight was more than the

Rapide's fully loaded weight.

Its first flight was shortly after VJ Day, and it was the first British transport aircraft to have propellers with reversible pitch. By the time production ended some 22 years later, 542 had rolled out of the de Havilland factory, not a huge number by wartime standards but making its presence felt in many countries. As the de Havilland Dove it was made in several versions, mainly differing in power and offering up to 380 hp each side but also with a number of cabin layouts, from 11 passengers to executive models seating five in considerable comfort. For the American market it was known as the Dove 8A or Dove Custom 800, and a Riley conversion fitted it with two 400 hp Lycoming engines.

The Dove name was hardly suitable for a military aircraft, so for air force use the DH104 became a Devon C.1, while the Royal Navy operated a number of Sea Devon C.20s for the light communications role. Many were exported to Commonwealth air forces and the RNZAF, for example, operated 30 Devons from 1948 until the last were retired in 1981. The first two were modified Doves on the assembly line and used as VIP transports, while most were operated as navigation and signals trainers and communications aircraft.

Postwar the de Havilland company was noted for its innovation. Following the Dove/Devon was the DH106 Comet, the world's first jet-powered passenger airliner and, unlike its Boeing rival, developed without the backing of a military equivalent. The DH108 tailless transonic research aircraft, although it crashed in September 1946 killing Geoffrey de Havilland, the son of the company's founder, provided valuable information for the aircraft which followed. Later fighters included the DH110 Sea Vixen and DH112 Venom, but one of the last de Havilland designs to appear before the company merged into the Hawker Siddeley Group was another small piston-engine airliner.

• de Havilland DH104 Devon	
Manufacturer:	The de Havilland Aircraft Company
Type:	Light transport
Engines:	Two de Havilland Gipsy Queen 70-3 6-cylinder inverted, air cooled, 345 hp
Wingspan:	57 ft ....17.37 m
Length:	39 ft 4 in..................12 m
Height:	13 ft 4 in..................4.06 m
Empty weight:	5725 lb ....2596 kg
Max loaded:	8800 lb ....3991 kg
Max range:	1070 miles ....1722 km
Max speed:	210 mph..................338 km/h
First flight:	25 September 1945
In production:	1946-1967

The DH114 Heron was first flown in May 1950, basically a development of the DH104 Dove and using as many of its components as possible, but lengthened to seat 14-17 passengers and fitted with four 250 hp Gipsy Queen 30 Mk 2 engines. Emphasis on simplicity resulted in a fixed undercarriage, but the Series 2 two years later had retractable gear to give 20 mph more cruise speed at the expense of a passenger's equivalent in weight. Almost 150 Herons were made and exported for civil and military use to some 30 countries, but by now all military examples have been retired.

This Heron served with the Queen's Flight at RAF Benson from 1958 to 1972 when it was transferred to the Fleet Air Arm as a Sea Heron VIP transport. As it was used to transport the Flag Officer Naval Air Command (FONAC) it was affectionately known as "The Admiral's Barge" and is seen here off the south coast of England just prior to its retirement in December 1989, being flown by Lt Cdr Tom Mason. *Gordon Bain*

DE HAVILLAND CANADA DHC-2 BEAVER

Ageing electrical systems can mean a spot of Armstrong starting, but Glenn Thompson, who grew up among topdressing Beavers, shows it's no big deal. *John King*

Once the Chipmunk design was well under way at the end of World War 2, work started on the next project at de Havilland Canada's factory at Downsview, Ontario. The idea was one which had been on the team's mind for some years.

With its population scattered across a vast wilderness, connected by few roads away from the southern belt, air transport in Canada was a vital necessity. Ground travel was difficult in the harsh winter, but in some ways the intense cold made air travel more straightforward as it offered the use of countless thousands of lakes and stretches of river, snow-covered, frozen solid and making ideal level landing grounds for aircraft on skis. Settlements tended to be near lakes and rivers and their traditional water-borne transport, often with airstrips handy, so with a combination of wheels and floats in summer and skis in winter the aircraft reigned supreme for quick transport.

The only problem was which aircraft. Prewar de Havilland types used in Canada included the DH61 Giant Moth of the 1920s and the DH83 Fox Moth of the 1930s, but both were fragile wood-and-fabric biplanes. The company resurrected the Fox Moth, which was effectively little more than a Tiger Moth with a small cabin in place of the open front cockpit, and made around 50 for postwar use. But what was needed was the proverbial half-ton truck, although little choice was available and the market was wide open for a new type.

The Ontario Department of Lands and Forests had long worked closely with The de Havilland Aircraft of Canada Ltd, from the first days of DH60 Moths on floats. During the war years the Department's pilots had been using Stinson SR-9 gullwing monoplanes as their basic bush equipment, but the type had some structural weaknesses, mostly the tendency to shed wings, which showed up as a result of pounding on floats. The Department approached both Fairchild and DH Canada with verbal offers to buy 25 aircraft if they met requirements, which included wings not coming off, and work started at the beginning of 1947 on the all-metal DHC-2 Beaver, named for that hard-working Canadian native animal.

Ruggedness and simplicity were the order of the day, from the strong fixed tailwheel undercarriage, the load-bearing floor with fuel tanks underneath, to struts bracing the long, high aspect ratio wing. Wide-span slotted flaps and drooping ailerons achieved truly STOL performance and were operated by hydraulic hand pumps, the subject of much discussion at the time but an integral part of the Beaver's design and character.

The original engine choice was the de Havilland Gipsy Queen 50, a supercharged inverted 6-cylinder unit of 295 hp. That was considered to be less than adequate and was still undergoing development tests, however, so with the airframe design about two-thirds finalised the decision was made at Downsview to change to the Pratt & Whitney R-985. The radial engine was both powerful enough at 450 hp and available in large quantities, and today it would be hard to visualise the Beaver as anything other than a blunt-nosed, no-nonsense bush aeroplane with a radial in front.

Test Pilot Russ Bannock gave the Beaver its first flight in August 1947 and the Ontario Department of Lands and Forests took delivery of the first four pro-

• de Havilland Canada DHC-2 Beaver		
Manufacturer:	........The de Havilland Aircraft of Canada Ltd	
Type:	......................Light utility transport	
Engine:	....................One Pratt & Whitney R-985-AN-1 Wasp Junior 9-cylinder radial, air cooled, 450 hp	
Wingspan:	.............48 ft	........................14.63 m
Length:	...................30 ft 3 in	................9.22 m
Height:	...................9 ft	........................2.74 m
Empty weight:	........2850 lb	....................1293 kg
Max loaded:	..........5100 lb	....................2313 kg
Max range:	...........733 miles	...............1180 km
Max speed:	.............163 mph	.................262 km/h at 5000 ft
First flight:	..............16 August 1947	
In production:	1948-1967	

duction examples – of a total of 44 it received over the years – in April 1948. Military orders followed, and more than half the total production of 1657 went to the US Army and US Air Force, the first peacetime orders by US defence authorities outside the continental USA. L-20 Beavers saw service in many areas of conflict, including Korea and Vietnam.

One was operated on skis by the RNZAF in Antarctica from 1956 until its crash three years later, flying as far south as 85°S, a far higher latitude than the type could reach in the Canadian High Arctic. Some consideration was given to moving the production line from Toronto to Wellington, New Zealand, but output of the Canadian utility aircraft finally ceased in 1967 after a 20-year production life.

The original RNZAF Antarctic Beaver was destroyed in a glacier crash in 1959 and so the paintwork on this New Zealand Warbirds example is an exact replica. It is flown by Greg Bryham over an appropriate landscape in 1991 after a winter storm blanketed the South Island high country. *John King*

DOUGLAS C-47 DAKOTA

The New Zealand Warbirds C-47, flown here by Paul Radley over Lake Wanaka, is used to carry members to airshows around the country. *Philip Makanna*

One of the most significant aircraft of all time started out not as a military type but a civilian airliner. The Douglas DC-3's conversion to an unarmed military transport needed minimal work, mainly in the form of a strengthened cargo floor and double loading doors in the rear fuselage, and it was built under licence in Japan and the Soviet Union as well as its native USA. The versatility of this former airliner saw it used in all imaginable military transport roles and even, in Vietnam, as a minigun platform for suppressive fire on ground targets, more than 35 years after the type's first production.

The Douglas Aircraft Company started in 1921 in Santa Monica, California, later expanding to other factories in California, Oklahoma and Illinois. At first its products were fabric-covered biplanes typical of the day, but the company quickly earned a reputation and two of its four World Cruisers which set out in 1924 managed to circumnavigate the world in 175 days. Later Douglas designs were monoplanes, but the DC-1, made for TWA in response to the revolutionary all-metal Boeing 247, set a new trend in passenger airliners with its sleek lines, cantilever wing, neatly cowled radial engines, retractable undercarriage and all-metal monocoque construction.

The one and only DC-1 first flew in July 1933, and lengthened and more powerful production versions were DC-2s, carrying 14 passengers each. Another development had a wider and longer fuselage and longer wings, as American Airlines wanted a sleeper version for transcontinental routes. Seating up to 28 or sleeping 14, the DC-3 became the world's best-known airliner. Millions of passengers in almost every country of the Western world have had their first airline rides in DC-3s, most of them after the urgency of their wartime military use dwindled, and the type continues today in commercial and some military operations, almost 65 years after its first flight.

More than 400 DC-3s had been delivered by the time the USA entered the war, but it had already filled the need for a versatile military transport, called the Dakota by the British. By the time production ended in 1947, more than 10,000 DC-3s, C-47s and variants had been made by Douglas, plus about 2000 in the USSR. They were powered by a range of Wright Cyclone and Pratt & Whitney Twin Wasp engines of 1000-1200 hp and made such an important contribution to the war effort that General Eisenhower declared them to be one of the four most significant weapons of World War 2.

Anywhere there was a need for carrying cargo or troops, over long distances through the Pacific and over inhospitable terrain such as the China-Burma-India route over the Himalayas known as The Hump, C-47s carried their loads reliably and uncomplainingly. Sometimes those operations were marginal, particularly when the aircraft were inadvertently overloaded, but somehow they always seemed to cope.

Stories about the C-47/DC-3 abound, and there was even one recorded incident where a DC-2 wing was grafted on to the centre section of a damaged C-47, which was then flown out from its precarious position in the Dutch East Indies. Its pilots still hold it in high regard, even affection. Any group of pilots will happily reminisce about the type's foibles, about

those windshield and hatch leaks whenever it rained, dripping water on to their kneepads and obliterating their flight plans. They recall bad-weather approaches, sometimes staggering under ice the aircraft was never intended to carry but always getting in – back in the days when navigational and landing aids were rudimentary, if they existed at all.

Some C-47s stayed on in the world's air forces for decades after World War 2 finished, but most were retired into airline service. Many of today's major airlines were founded on the strengths and availability of Donald Douglas's DC-3, which grew into the C-47 and back into the DC-3 again. It is truly one of the world's greatest aircraft.

This C-47 is one of the few now wearing warpaint, and authenticity of finish extends to a weathered effect with the D-Day invasion stripes aiding visibility in New Zealand's predominantly green landscapes. Owned by a group of New Zealand Warbirds members, it is operated on regular scenic flights around its Auckland base and is flown here by Bob Tarr and Warwick Batten. *John King*

• Douglas C-47 Dakota		
Manufacturer:	........Douglas Aircraft Company	
Type:	......................Military transport	
Engines:	................Two Pratt & Whitney R-1830-92 Twin Wasp 14-cylinder radial, air cooled, 1200 hp	
Wingspan:	..............95 ft	........................28.96 m
Length:	...................64 ft 6 in	................19.66 m
Height:	..................16 ft 11½ in	.........5.16 m
Empty weight:	........17,720 lb	................8030 kg
Max loaded:	..........29,300 lb	...............13,290 kg
Max range:	............1510 miles	.............2430 km
Max speed:	............215 mph	.................346 km/h
First flight:	.............17 December 1935 (DC-3)	
In production:	1936-1947	

PIPER L-4A GRASSHOPPER

A minimal warbird, the L-4A nevertheless packed a punch out of all proportion to its size and weight.
John King

It may be the smallest, lowest-powered and by far the most modest of all the recognised warbirds, but the army liaison aircraft was described at the time as one of the three best innovations of World War 2. Used as air observation posts and for general communications duties, such light aircraft saw service in all the major theatres. While they have been largely ignored in many official histories, their contribution to the war effort was appreciated by all those who knew the true story.

The development of the idea was largely parallel in the minds of British and American army generals, away from the high-performance, armed army cooperation aircraft and towards something light, manoeuvrable and capable of being operated out of unprepared airstrips. But while the British focused on their Auster with its 130 hp Lycoming or Gipsy Major engine, the American standard had only half the power with consequently less ability.

By June 1941 the US Army had been persuaded of the merits of liaison aircraft and gathered light two-seaters from Piper, Taylorcraft and Aeronca for tests in Texas, Louisiana and the Carolinas. The sight of a dozen or so little aircraft bounding around the Texas semi-desert, all powered by 65 hp Continental engines, led Major General Innis P. Swift to describe them as 'grasshoppers', a name which became official for all three makes of the generic type. In the end the Piper L-4, a slightly modified J-3 Cub, won favour because of its docile handling qualities, and almost 7000 L-4s were made between 1942 and 1945. Taylorcraft L-2s numbered almost 2000 and Aeronca L-3s more than 1300, bringing the total Grasshopper production to more than 10,000.

Life for these smallest military aircraft was exciting. While the British Auster had plenty of power and a startling angle of climb, the L-4 was marginal in performance, particularly with two on board, and takeoff accidents accounted for the greatest number of losses, well ahead of those caused by enemy aircraft or ground fire while in flight. The very manoeuvrability of the Grasshopper, and the training emphasis given to very low flying and evasive actions, kept them out of the opposition's gunsights for the most part, although some did crash into trees, wires and haystacks while avoiding Bf 109s in Europe.

They were most useful following the Allied invasion of Europe, during the often confused fighting which marked the progress of the armies towards Germany. With their ability to operate from almost any field with reasonable approaches (and some without such advantages!), the Grasshoppers were based near the fluid front line and were able to pinpoint the enemy positions. Flying in sometimes appalling winter weather, their pilots often saved their own troops from surprise ambushes and called in air and artillery attacks on German soldiers and tanks, saving numerous Allied lives and earning unstinting praise.

Although they were unarmed, with occasional exceptions such as L-4H *Rosie the Rocketeer*, fitted with bazookas to its struts by Major Charles "Bazooka Charlie" Carpenter, the Grasshoppers were anything but harmless. No other class of aeroplane was able to rain down so much tonnage of high explosive with such accuracy, albeit indirectly, and it was no wonder they were the target of enemy guns and fighters.

After the end of hostilities in 1945 many surplus L-4s were retired to civilian life as inoffensive little J-3 Cubs. A number have kept their military identities and still more have been changed back, in recognition of the valuable part they played as the smallest and cheekiest warbirds.

Piper L-4A Grasshopper		
Manufacturer:	........Piper Aircraft Corporation	
Type:	......................Light communications/liaison aircraft	
Engine:	....................One Continental A-65-8 4-cylinder horizontally opposed, air cooled, 65 hp	
Wingspan:	.............35 ft 2½ in	..............10.7 m
Length:	....................22 ft 4½ in	..............6.82 m
Height:	...................6 ft 8 in	...................2.03 m
Empty weight:	........740 lb	......................336 kg
Max loaded:	..........1170 lb	...................530 kg
Max range:	.............190 miles	................306 km
Max speed:	.............85 mph	..................137 km/h at sea level
First flight:	.............1938 (J-3)	
In production:	1942-1945	

Like its British Auster equivalent, the Grasshopper spent most of its working life at low levels. This 1942 example never flew in anger, but was stationed in Hawaii and was civilianised as a J-3 Cub after the war. Unused after 1963, it became derelict and was brought to New Zealand in the late 1980s to be restored and flown again in 1994. Gilly Smith flies her L-4A near its base north of Auckland. *John King*

Avro 683 Lancaster

Only two Lancasters are airworthy and fewer than 10 are preserved in museums around the world. This Mk 7 was made in 1945 at the Austin works, Longbridge, and went to the French in 1950. After service as a maritime patrol and reconnaissance aircraft based in the Pacific it was presented to the Museum of Transport & Technology, Auckland, in April 1964.

Members of the RAF Bomber Command Association (NZ) have restored the Lancaster in the museum over many years and it is almost completely fitted out with appropriate equipment. Seated at the wireless operator's position (left) is Des Andrewes (actually a 622 Squadron navigator), with Alan Wiltshire (75, 550 and 207 Squadrons) on the navigator's bench and Des Hall (flight engineer with 463 RAAF Squadron) looking round from the pilot's seat. *John King*

Not many renowned aircraft derive, not greatly changed, from an unsuccessful predecessor, but Avro's heavy bomber, one of the success stories of World War 2 and one of the greatest and most influential aircraft of all time, did just that. A total of 7377 Lancasters were produced, including 430 built in Canada by Victory Aircraft, and it was adapted to drop almost all the types of bombs which the busy wartime boffins could invent, including the Barnes Wallis skipping bomb, and in weight all the way up to the 22,000 pound Grand Slam or Earthquake bomb. Whatever somebody thought up in the way of high explosive to be dropped on targets, mostly in Europe, the Lancaster was able to deliver it.

British bombers were named after cities such as Halifax, Stirling and Warwick, and Avro's Manchester was something of a departure for the company. During the 1920s and first half of the 1930s A.V. Roe was noted for its series of excellent light biplanes and civil passenger aircraft, originally the licence-built Fokker F.VIIB/3m but developed into its own range. The all-metal Manchester was much larger and heavier than anything previously emerging from the drawing boards of Roy Chadwick and his design team.

When Rolls-Royce announced its intention in 1935 to produce the Vulture, a very powerful X-24 engine based on two sets of Peregrine V-12 cylinder blocks on a common crankcase, the Air Ministry issued specification P.13/36 for a twin-engine heavy bomber. Handley Page changed at an early stage to four Rolls-Royce Merlins for its Halifax, but Avro persevered with the Vulture, to its regret. Seriously down on power and suffering from unreliability even at derated power settings, the engine was a failure and plans to build the Manchester in quantity were cancelled. Only 209 were delivered and all surviving examples were withdrawn from service in June 1942 and scrapped.

The airframe showed a great deal of promise, so back at the drawing board in 1940 Chadwick designed a longer-span wing with four Merlin engines. He used much of the existing Manchester structure and in fact the first batch of Lancasters had Manchester fuselages already under construction, and the new bomber was immediately put into large-scale production.

Its first operational sortie was a daylight raid on 17 April 1942, but for the next two years Lancasters flew mostly night missions over Europe before reverting to daylight flights. In 156,000 sorties they dropped more than 608,000 tonnes of bombs, and one Lancaster survived about 150 trips. The second-scoring example, R5868 with 140-plus sorties, is preserved in the Bomber Command Museum, Hendon.

Avro Lancaster

Manufacturer:	A.V. Roe Ltd
Type:	Long-range heavy bomber
Engines:	Four Rolls-Royce Merlin 20 or 22 V-12 cylinder, liquid cooled, 1460 hp
Wingspan:	102 ft ...... 31.09 m
Length:	69 ft 6 in ...... 21.2 m
Height:	19 ft 7 in ...... 5.7 m
Empty weight:	36,900 lb ...... 16,738 kg
Max loaded:	68,000 lb ...... 30,845 kg
Max range:	2230 miles ...... 3589 km
Max speed:	287 mph ...... 462 km/h at 11,500 ft
First flight:	9 January 1941
In production:	1941-1946

Loads carried in the long bomb bay were varied, from the standard selection of bombs weighing a total of 14,000 pounds to specialist weapons. Lancasters of No. 617 (Dambusters) Squadron were used to drop the Wallis spinning drum skip bombs on the Ruhr Valley dams, and others flew with 12,000 pound and even the 22,000 pound Earthquake bomb. The Lancaster was used to lift heavier loads of bigger bombs than any other aircraft in the European theatre and its survival rate was comparatively high, with 132 tonnes dropped for every aircraft lost (the Stirling, the worst example, dropped only 41 tonnes). Towards the end of the war Lancasters were used in the battlefield close support role and later dropped supplies throughout Europe and ferried home former prisoners of war.

The Canadian Warplane Heritage's Lancaster is flown near Galveston, Texas, with Stewart Brickenden and Don Fisher at the controls. *Philip Makanna*

BOEING B-17 FLYING FORTRESS

Lone Star's B-17G is flown by Ralph Royce out of Galveston, Texas. *Philip Makanna*

Not made in such large numbers –12,731 in total – as some other heavy bombers and not carrying an exceptional bomb load, the B-17 nevertheless had an enviable reputation and was always at the forefront of American bombing efforts, in Europe and all other theatres of war. A combination of high-altitude capability and a capacity to absorb battle damage endeared it to its aircrews, but more important historically was its role in the daylight strategic assault on Germany, despite fierce political argument and in the face of desperate enemy opposition.

Boeing set a trend in 1933 with its Model 247 airliner, an all-metal cantilever monoplane with twin engines and retractable undercarriage which made its rivals suddenly obsolete. The company had long built military fighters and bombers, and the USAAC in 1934, having temporarily won an argument with the US Navy over the ascendancy of aircraft over ships for coastal defence, issued a requirement for a bomber with a very long 5000 mile range at 200 mph, carrying a bomb load of 2000 pounds. Boeing's response under the leadership of Edward C. Wells was the Model 294, a very large four-engine bomber which flew in prototype form as the XBLR-1, later changed to XB-15.

While that project proceeded no further, the wing and engines were used on the 314 Clipper long-range civil flying boat and the Boeing team started work on another, smaller, multi-engine bomber as a private venture. Boeing stayed with four engines when most of its contemporaries were powered by two, and the new Model 299 shared the 247's structural and aerodynamic principles, with a large wing spanning more than 100 feet and circular fuselage with tall and graceful fin and rudder.

Boeing invested heavily in the belief that its product would be irresistible, and less than a month after the B-299's first test flight it was flown to Wright Field for USAAC evaluation, covering the 2100 miles nonstop at more than 230 mph. Its destruction in a crash after takeoff two months later near the end of the trials, although shown to have been caused by inadvertently leaving the controls locked and no fault of the aircraft, did the new bomber no good in the eyes of officialdom. Plans to order 65 were dropped and only the 13 evaluation YB-17s were made as the different factions, USAAC strategic air power versus US Navy tactical warfare, continued to argue their cases in Washington. In 1938 the Secretary of War directed the USAAC to procure only light, medium and attack bombers.

But the Munich crisis provided the impetus for further thoughts about heavy bombers and an order was placed for 39 production B-17Bs, the first to be fitted with turbo-supercharged Wright Cyclone engines for performance at altitude. Twenty B-17Cs went to the RAF for operational use over Europe, which led to the improved B-17D and -E versions with revised armament, armour and self-sealing tanks.

The B-17E also introduced the definitive profile with deeper rear fuselage and a much larger fin and rudder for better bombing accuracy at altitude, as well as more defensive guns and the powered dorsal and ventral turrets which started to make the B-17 live up to its Fortress name. Some went to reinforce existing groups in the Pacific, and the first six B-17Es to arrive in Java in January 1942 inflicted heavy damage on the approaching Japanese invasion fleet.

B-17s were used in all theatres of World War 2 and are probably most famous for the massed daylight bombing raids over Germany and occupied Europe. The type is the Americans' favourite bomber, just as the Lancaster is to the British, and its place in history is assured.

This B-17G was built at Long Beach, California, by the Douglas Aircraft Company and served after the war with Air/Sea 1st Rescue Squadron and later with MATS. During April 1952 it was instrumented and exposed to the effects of three different nuclear explosions, then disposed of for scrap in 1965, but work started on restoration to flying condition as *Yucca Lady*. After use as a fire bomber, dropping water and borate, the B-17G had a major restoration and was painted to represent *Nine-O-Nine* of the 91st Bomb Group, 323rd Squadron. Yet another rebuild was necessary after a landing accident in 1987, and the aircraft is now back on the airshow circuit touring the USA in company with B-24J, N224J. *Gordon Bain*

• Boeing B-17G Flying Fortress	
Manufacturer:	........Boeing Aircraft Company
Type:	......................Long-range heavy bomber
Engines:	.................Four Wright Cyclone R-1820-97 9-cylinder radial, air cooled, 1200 hp
Wingspan:	..............103 ft 9 in ....31.62 m
Length:	...................74 ft 3 in ....22.66 m
Height:	...................19 ft 1 in ....5.8 m
Empty weight:	........36,135 lb................16,391 kg
Max loaded:	..........65,000 lb................29,484 kg
Max range:	.............3400 miles..............5472 km
Max speed:	.............287 mph ....462 km/h at 25,000 ft
First flight:	..............28 July 1935
In production:	1939-1945

Boeing B-29 Superfortress

Philip Makanna

Not many aircraft types could be said to end one era and usher in another, but the B-29, the long-range high-altitude pressurised bomber, did just that. Boeing's Model 345 Superfortress is most famous – or infamous – for being the type used to drop the atomic bombs on Hiroshima and Nagasaki in August 1945, ending World War 2 and heralding the Atomic Age which developed into the Cold War with its constant threat of nuclear weapons.

But the B-29 was much more than the first, and so far only, bomber to drop nuclear weapons in anger. The almost 4000 examples built by Boeing, Bell and Martin between September 1943 and May 1946, a remarkable production effort in itself, dropped 171,060 tons of conventional bombs on Japanese territory, compared with 6,781 tons by all other aircraft combined. Some were modified to carry British 22,000 pound Earthquake or Grand Slam bombs, one under each inner wing, although such a 44,000 pound load was never dropped operationally.

B-29s were used in the Asia-Pacific theatre, at first against Bangkok from bases in India but mostly bombing Japan. Before they could operate from bases in China they had to carry their squadrons' own fuel supplies, seven tons at a time, over the Hump, across the Himalaya Mountains. Once the Mariana Islands had been captured, massive airfields were constructed

and Superfortresses started bombing the Japanese homeland from there in November 1944, systematically destroying the country's industrial cities.

Bigger and far in advance of anything else the Americans had ever built, the B-29 bristled with new features. Technical problems, as well as almost 900 design changes called for by the USAAC and USAAF (the Air Corps became an Air Force in June 1941), were overcome with a massive effort and a production organisation involving Boeing, Bell, North American, Fisher (General Motors) and later Martin. In engine power, gross weight, wing loading, basic structure, pressurisation and armament the Superfortress set entirely new standards and a six-fold increase in technology over any earlier bomber.

The B-29's genesis was a 1938 study for a pressurised bomber with tricycle undercarriage, longer range, higher speed and heavier bomb load for truly intercontinental operations. Proposals firmed during the following year until Specification XC-218 was issued, closely matching work that Boeing had been doing, and the company won the contract ahead of Douglas, Lockheed and Consolidated.

That was just the start of the work, and not only on the airframe and systems. The engine chosen was the 18-cylinder Wright R-3350, turbo-supercharged and producing 2200 hp on takeoff, but in mid-1940 only one example existed and the subsequent speed of development and production was to cause its own problems.

Enormous flaps of almost one-sixth the wing area brought takeoff and landing speeds to reasonable levels with such a high wing loading, and flush riveting of wings and fuselage gave the aerodynamic efficiency needed for speed and height. Different parts of the fuselage were pressurised, with the control cabin and gunners' central area connected by a crawl tunnel crossing above the unpressurised bomb bay. The rear gunner sat all alone with his 20 mm cannon and two 0.5 inch machine guns, unconnected to anybody

else except by intercom. Apart from the tail unit, the guns had a central control system with a computer which could automatically correct for range, altitude, speed and temperature. The gunners, one in the nose and two amidships, were physically removed from their weapons and could switch control of the two forward, dorsal and ventral turrets between themselves.

Such a powerful strategic bomber served with the USAF and the RAF (as well as the Soviet Air Force with Tu-4 copies) for a number of years after the war, and the B-50 was essentially the same aircraft with four Pratt & Whitney R-4360 engines. Several B-29s still exist today, but their size and complexity make them a rare sight in the air, the largest of all active warbirds.

By far the largest, heaviest and most complex of the World War 2 bombers was the B-29, today one of the rarest of all flying warbirds. The Confederate Air Force example is seen near Oakland, California, with Tom Cloyd at the controls. *Philip Makanna*

• Boeing B-29A Superfortress		
Manufacturer:	........Boeing Airplane Company	
Type:	......................Long-range high-altitude heavy bomber	
Engines:	................Four Wright Cyclone R-3350-23 18-cylinder radial, air cooled, 2200 hp	
Wingspan:	..............142 ft 3 in	..............43.35 m
Length:	...................99 ft	........................30.18 m
Height:	...................27 ft 9 in	.................8.46 m
Empty weight:	........71,360 lb	.................32,369 kg
Max loaded:	...........138,500 lb	...............62,823 kg
Max range:	.............4100 miles	.............6598 km
Max speed:	.............358 mph at 25,000 ft	.................576 km/h
First flight:	.............September 1942	
In production:	1943-1946	

BRISTOL TYPE 142M BLENHEIM

Fast and sleek for its time, the Bristol Blenheim was Britain's first modern all-metal stressed-skin monoplane with retractable undercarriage and flaps, but it was soon overtaken by developing technology. *Philip Makanna*

Many excellent service aircraft have started as either civil commercial types or private ventures by manufacturers who could see a gap in their countries' materiel. Going out on their own, they developed aircraft which the authorities sometimes had trouble accepting, as in the case of the de Havilland Mosquito, but usually the result was so obvious that specifications were written around them and promising aircraft were put into production.

The Bristol Aeroplane Company started in 1910 at Bristol, Somerset, and was noted for its range of biplane fighters into the 1930s. None of its previous output, however, gave any hint of the capabilities of the twin-engine executive aircraft Bristol designed for the newspaper magnate Lord Rothermere, based on the Type 135 mockup displayed at the 1934 Salon International de l'Aéronautique in Paris. Built to carry a pilot and six passengers, the Type 142 was the country's first modern all-metal stressed-skin cantilever monoplane with retractable undercarriage, flaps and, shortly afterwards, variable pitch propellers. When it reached 307 mph on an Air Ministry test, after Lord Rothermere had named it *Britain First* and presented it to the Air Council,

its performance surprised even its designer, Frank Barnwell. The civil aircraft was fully 30 mph faster than any fighter the RAF had at the time.

Naturally enough, the RAF wanted something with such speed, so the Bristol design team came up with a new fuselage, carrying a crew of three and slightly deeper than the first, with a mid-mounted wing to give room for a bomb bay beneath. Such a technical advance over all previous British military aircraft eased the disquiet felt at the RAF's increasingly obsolescent equipment, but the Blenheim and its Bisley and Bolingbroke derivatives never quite lived up to the high hopes placed in them.

In that way the Blenheim echoed the Curtiss P-40 fighter, both praised and vilified. Both aircraft led the way and were excellent examples of the technology of the time, but they were soon overtaken through no fault of their designers or manufacturers.

The Blenheim had its shortcomings, notably lack of defensive armament and armour, and was unduly vulnerable to fighter attack. Still, it was made in large numbers – more than 5300 of all versions – and exported to six other European air arms, bearing the brunt of the first years of World War 2 fighting. Blenheims served with all RAF Commands, Bomber, Fighter, Coastal, Training and Army Cooperation, and were effective in the Western Desert and in the defence of Burma and Malaya as well as against shipping in the North Sea.

A major recognition feature of the Blenheim Mk I was its short, blunt nose, but work started early on a conversion, the Bolingbroke, which had the windscreen moved forward three feet, better to accommodate the navigator/bomb aimer and his table. Since the pilot's position was unchanged that meant inadequate vision for him, so the windscreen was moved back to its original position and the forward transparencies on his side scalloped to give a better sight line for takeoff and landing. Canadian production of the new version by Vickers was all named

Bolingbroke, but the revised bomber, made in England by Bristol, A.V. Roe and Rootes Securities, became the Blenheim Mk IV, the RAF's main combat version.

Production of all Blenheims stopped in 1943 as the type had been made obsolescent by newer bombers. As the RAF's main bomber on the outbreak of war, the Blenheim paved the way for daylight operations over enemy territory, and Bristol went on to produce some extremely effective aircraft, including the Beaufighter. But a direct and inevitable result of a steep learning curve in military aircraft and operations is a high casualty rate, and the Blenheim is not rated in history as highly as it deserves.

After the disastrous crash of his first rebuilt Blenheim at Denham, Graham Warner decided to proceed with a second project. John Romain's company was the principal rebuilder at Duxford and he is flying it here in the colours of L8841 of 254 Squadron. *Gordon Bain*

• Bristol Blenheim Mk IV		
Manufacturer:	........Bristol Aeroplane Company	
Type:	......................Medium bomber	
Engines:	.................Two Bristol Mercury XV 9-cylinder radial, air cooled, 905 hp	
Wingspan:	..............56 ft 4 in	.................17.17 m
Length:	....................42 ft 7 in	.................12.98 m
Height:	....................12 ft 10 in	..............3.91 m
Empty weight:	........9790 lb	...................4440 kg
Max loaded:	...........14,400 lb	.................6530 kg
Max range:	.............1460 miles	.............2350 km
Max speed:	.............266 mph	.................428 km/h at 11,800 ft
First flight:	..............25 June 1936	
In production:	1937-1943	

CONSOLIDATED PBY-5A CATALINA

This Catalina, now owned and flown by a Confederate Air Force group and seen here with Pete Ettinger at the controls, was once a forest fire water bomber.
Philip Makanna

Consolidated's twin-engine maritime patrol bomber is often dubbed the most famous flying boat of them all. The claim has some substance, with more than 4000 of the type built in the USA, Canada and the Soviet Union over a 10-year production life, and the PBY and its derivatives served with the forces of all Allied countries during World War 2. It has earned its place in history.

Like so many warplanes, the Catalina had two quite separate faces and was either mightily welcomed or feared, depending on which side you were on. Pleased to see them were all the ditched aircrew, bobbing in liferafts or lifejackets and rescued by PBYs from waters all over the world, including some daring open-ocean efforts. But anybody aboard a submarine had much to fear from the 2000 pounds of bombs, depth charges or other stores carried under the wings of a Catalina.

In 1933 the US Navy issued specifications for a new twin-engine cantilever monoplane flying boat, more modern than any of the biplane designs which had previously appeared. Both Douglas and

Consolidated vied for the contract, but Consolidated, which tended to specialise in marine aircraft in the early 1930s, was successful. Its product, designed by Isaac M. 'Mac' Laddon, went on to be made in higher numbers than any other flying boat, but only a handful of the 80 or so surviving examples remain airworthy.

Laddon's XP3Y-1 design had a massive parasol wing mounted atop a central pylon and braced by two struts on each side. Although all the structure was metal, the trailing one-third of the wing was fabric covered, having no flaps or aerodynamic additions but with the stabilising floats retracting outwards to become the wingtips in flight. The Pratt & Whitney Twin Wasp radial engines were mounted close to the centre line with the propellers just behind the cockpit, and the flight engineer's station was in the central pylon. The hull was beamier than it was tall and later versions had a large blister canopy on each side, behind the wing and above the aft step, for crew access, defensive machine guns or hoisting downed airmen out of the water.

The unprecedented (for a maritime aircraft) number of 60 PBY-1s was ordered in 1935, soon followed by a further 50 PBY-2s which differed only in detail. In 1938 the PBY-3 was cleared for export and three went to the USSR, where the type was promptly put into production in Taganrog. The RAF placed large orders in 1939 and called the flying boat the Catalina, a name later adopted by the USA, but the biggest change came in April 1939.

A PBY-4 was returned to the manufacturer and converted into an amphibian. The nosewheel retracted into a well covered by automatically operating hatches, while the main gear, fitted with oleo shock absorbers, retracted into wells in the fuselage sides. The resulting PBY-5A was called the Canso by the RCAF, but all versions, flying boat and amphibian, are known today by the generic name Catalina. Some were inevitably modified back to PBY-5 standard, without wheels.

• Consolidated PBY-5A Catalina		
Manufacturer:	........Consolidated Aircraft Corporation	
Type:	........Long-range maritime patrol bomber flying boat	
Engines:	........Two Pratt & Whitney R-1830-92 Twin Wasp 14-cylinder radial, air cooled, 1200 hp	
Wingspan:	........104 ft	........37.10 m
Length:	........63 ft 10 in	........19.47 m
Height:	........20 ft 2 in	........6.15 m
Empty weight:	........20,910 lb	........9483 kg
Max loaded:	........35,300 lb	........16,008 kg
Max range:	........2990 miles	........4812 km
Cruise speed:	........117 mph at sea level	........188 km/h
First flight:	........21 March 1935	
In production:	1936-1945	

The Catalina's war record was remarkable. It was widely rumoured to climb at 90 knots, cruise at 90 knots and land at 90 knots, only a slight exaggeration, but its endurance of more than 20 hours saw it over some far-flung parts of the oceans.

In peacetime they were still used by many air forces and navies, as well as airlines to survey routes across the Pacific Ocean, but most were scrapped and the numbers dwindled. Activity was prolonged by their use as water bombers, fighting forest fires, and a select few have been converted into aerial yachts. Others are maintained as warbirds and the drone of the twin Pratt & Whitneys, marking a Catalina's stately progress across the sky, is likely to be heard for a long time to come.

The PBY-5A Catalina owned and operated by a New Zealand Warbirds group, and flown here by Chris Snelson and Tony Butcher, passes over Hobsonville, Auckland, for many years the centre of all the RNZAF's flying boat operations. *John King*

CONSOLIDATED MODEL 32 B-24 LIBERATOR

Gordon Bain

Several bomber types have become famous, sometimes for rather esoteric reasons. The British Lancaster and the American B-17 Fortress and B-25 Mitchell have all earned their fame, whether for dropping special bombs, featuring in particularly daring raids or simply for having books written or films made about them. All excellent aircraft in their own right, they have become known for reasons outside their original intentions.

And yet the most noteworthy of all bombers has never known such popular fame. Made in greater numbers than any other American aircraft and in more versions for more purposes, distinctive in its appearance, the most complicated and expensive aircraft seen up to that time, the B-24 Liberator served with the air arms of 15 Allied nations in every World War 2 theatre. But no famous movies have been made about the Liberator to make audiences misty-eyed and no popular books have been written to star this most significant aircraft. Fame can be a fickle thing.

The Liberator had similar power and weight to the B-17 which preceded it by five years, but in performance and weight-carrying capability it was no better. In stability, particularly engine-out control, it was a handful for the average pilot, but its versatility

and range made it the favoured bomber for varied roles with many countries.

Its distinctive shape, with a deep fuselage, was governed by the use of the Davis wing, a high-aspect ratio wing of unusual length and narrow chord. Its aerodynamic forte was high efficiency in the cruise which, combined with large fuel capacity, gave the B-24 its unusually long range and allowed anti-submarine operations far out into the Atlantic Ocean, an area previously unpatrolled and so a favourite for U-boat packs. The wing's carry-through centre-section structure, effectively making it a one-piece unit, dictated its position as a high shoulder wing with long, outward retracting undercarriage, and the tall bomb bay beneath. Access to the disposable armament was through roll-up doors, with up to 8000 pounds of bombs hung vertically either side of a central catwalk. Two 4000 pound bombs could be slung outside on inner-wing racks.

The Liberator had twin fins and rudders, but the final transport versions used by the US Army, US Navy and RAF had an extremely tall single fin, a feature carried through to the PB4Y Privateer. That 1943 long-range oversea patrol bomber development of the Liberator used the same Davis wing with a longer fuselage and changed armament and internal arrangements, but its performance was lower because of the extra weight of airframe and equipment.

More than 19,000 B-24s in their many variants were produced between 1939, when the prototype first flew just before the end of the year, and the shutting down of the factories in May 1945. As well as the parent Consolidated Vultee (Convair) production, Liberators were also made by Douglas, Ford and North American Aviation, more than half the final total being the definitive B-24G, H and J versions. The type also appeared as the C-87 Liberator Express transport, TB-24 trainer, F-7 photo reconnaissance, C-109 fuel tanker and QB-24 drone, plus the CB-24 lead ship.

Probably the best-known Liberator operation was the August 1943 raid by B-24Ds of the 44th, 93rd,

98th and 389th Bomb Groups on the Ploesti oil refinery in Romania, which had been supplying Germany with its vital oil and fuel. The mission was successful, as were so many of the other operations in which Liberators took part, but otherwise this remarkable bomber had a largely unremarked career.

Despite being made in the highest numbers, the B-24 is one of the rarest of World War 2 bombers. Only two are currently airworthy, the B-24A operated by the Confederate Air Force and the B-24J of the Collings Foundation of Stow, Massachusetts, seen here in June 1995 over the Golden Gate Bridge, San Francisco, flown by Jon Rising.

This B-24J served with the RAF in the Pacific until the war ended, when it was abandoned at Khanpur in India, then from 1948 until it was again retired in 1968 it flew with the Indian Air Force.

The *All American* is named after a 461st Bomb Group aircraft serving with the 15th Air Force which was lost over Yugoslavia on 4 October 1944. All of the crew survived. *Philip Makanna*

• Consolidated B-24J Liberator	
Manufacturer:	Consolidated Vultee Aircraft Corporation
Type:	Long-range heavy bomber
Engines:	Four Pratt & Whitney R-1830-65 Twin Wasp 14-cylinder radial, air cooled, 1200 hp
Wingspan:	110 ft .... 33.53 m
Length:	67 ft 2 in .... 20.47 m
Height:	18 ft .... 5.49 m
Empty weight:	36,500 lb .... 16,556 kg
Max loaded:	65,000 lb .... 29,484 kg
Max range:	2100 miles .... 3379 km
Max speed:	290 mph .... 467 km/h at 25,000 ft
First flight:	December 1939
In production:	1940-1945

DE HAVILLAND DH98 MOSQUITO

Mosquito RR299 was built at Leavesden in March 1945 as one of a batch of 50 and was transferred to 27 MU during March 1963 and then acquired by Hawker Siddeley Aviation, as G-ASKH, four months later. It is seen here on 17 July 1983 with BAe test pilot Tony Craig in command. *Gordon Bain*

With the benefit of hindsight it is hard to fathom today why the idea of the Mosquito, one of the most brilliantly innovative and effective aircraft of World War 2, took so long to be accepted in official circles. True, it was made entirely of wood when all military aircraft were tending towards metal, and the proposal that it should be an unarmed light bomber in the hope that it would outrun the fast German fighters known to exist was very hard to take seriously. But the potential was always there, if only Air Ministry officials had seen it earlier – and an earlier acceptance would have seen a higher production run and perhaps altered the course of World War 2.

Fortunately for all concerned, Geoffrey de Havilland and his colleagues were persistent. The de Havilland Aircraft Company started work on the Mosquito as a private venture in October 1938, using wood because of the strain on Britain's supply of essential metals and also because small sections could be made by carpenters in widely dispersed locations.

No British aircraft company understood wooden construction methods better than de Havilland, which until that time had produced only one major aircraft of stressed-skin all-metal structure, the DH95

Flamingo. Its 1937 DH91 Albatross, arguably the most elegantly streamlined airliner of all time, had a monocoque fuselage built of cedar ply laminated around a core of balsa wood and strengthened by rigid bulkheads and spruce stringers, and the same method was used for the Mosquito.

The idea did not appeal to the people from the Air Ministry, who suggested that de Havilland's Hatfield plant would be better employed making wings for existing heavy bombers. But persistence, and the outbreak of war, won the day and a contract was awarded for 50 aircraft on 1 March 1940. Some months later the Hatfield factory was destroyed by bombs, but the Mosquito prototype was being built in secrecy at Salisbury Hall and, painted yellow, first flew on 25 November 1940, with outstanding results.

Still the Ministry dithered, and the first operational sortie of the new type took place only in September 1941. A solitary unarmed reconnaissance model took a series of photographs of the French Atlantic coast and had no trouble outrunning the Bf 109 fighters sent to intercept it. The idea was proved sound by the return of an enthusiastic pilot and the idea of the Mosquito was at last gaining general acceptance.

Powered by two Rolls-Royce Merlin engines, the Mosquito had the minimum airframe needed to support and control more than 2500 hp, and careful streamlining and attention to detail resulted in a top speed of more than 400 mph. Production in England, Canada and Australia resulted in a total of 7781 aircraft in numerous variants, from unarmed photographic reconnaissance to naval torpedo carrier, and at the extreme opposite end of the performance scale to the Fairey Swordfish.

Most were either bombers or fighters, or a combination of the two. The bomber at first carried four 500 pound bombs in its internal bomb bay, but continual development led to the definitive version which had a pressurised cockpit and enlarged bomb bay to hold a 4000 pound weapon, as big as the original load

de Havilland DH98 Mosquito Mk XVI	
Manufacturer:	The de Havilland Aircraft Company
Type:	Two-seat high-speed day-night fighter-bomber
Engines:	Two Rolls-Royce Merlin 21 V-12 cylinder, liquid cooled, 1280 hp
Wingspan:	54 ft 2 in ... 16.5 m
Length:	40 ft 6 in ... 12.34 m
Height:	15 ft 3½ in ... 4.66 m
Empty weight:	15,900 lb ... 7210 kg
Max loaded:	25,000 lb ... 11,340 kg
Normal range:	1860 miles ... 2990 km
Max speed:	410 mph ... 660 km/h
First flight:	25 November 1940
In production:	1941-1949

carried by the much larger Lancaster. The night fighter, which first flew in May 1941 with pilot and observer sitting side-by-side, was armed with four 20 mm Hispano cannon under the cockpit floor and four 0.303 in Browning machine guns in the nose. The fighter-bomber also had two crew and the same armament, but also carried two 250 pound bombs in the rear bay and an assortment of bombs, mines, depth charges or rockets on wing racks.

Its exploits were legion, but its most famous were low-level surprise attacks. One such sortie destroyed the German Gestapo headquarters in Oslo, Norway, and another broke down the walls of the prison at Amiens, France, where hundreds of resistance fighters were awaiting imminent execution.

Deterioration of wood and glues over time has meant that few examples survive, but the prototype is preserved at its birthplace, Salisbury Hall, and others can be found in museums in several countries.

Kermit Weeks flies his Mosquito from his base in Florida. *Philip Makanna*

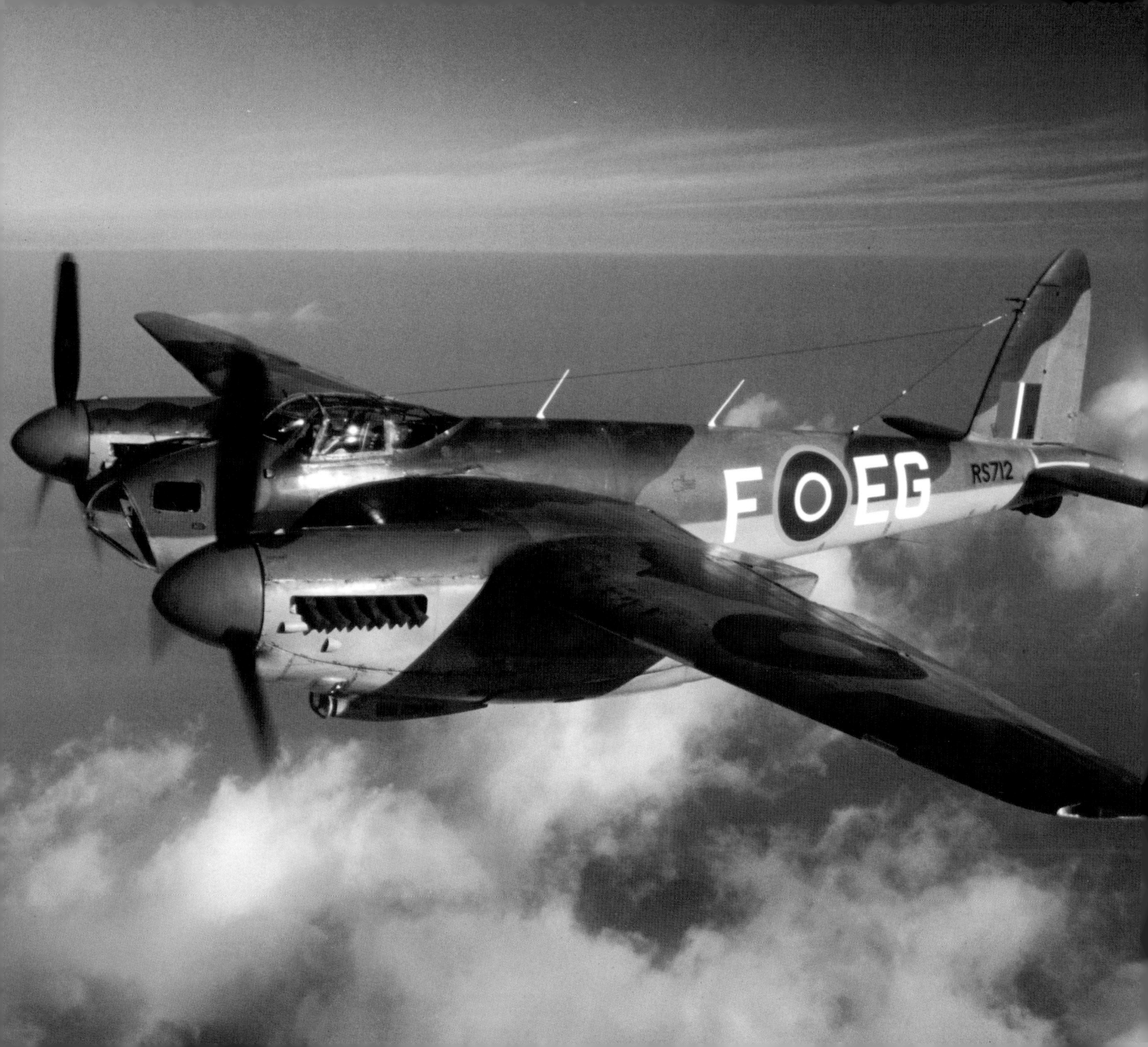
F EG
RS712

Douglas A-26 Invader

Although *Feeding Frenzy* was built in 1944, as 44-34588, it did not see action during World War 2. It did, however, serve in Korea and then French Indo-China after being leased to the French Armée de l'Air.

After its retirement from active duty it was purchased by the Hughes Aircraft Corporation for use as a missile radar guidance testbed. At the time of the photograph with Bruce Guberman at the controls in May 1994 it was based at Burbank, California, where it was owned by Bill Timmer. *Gordon Bain*

The Douglas Aircraft Company was best known during the 1930s for its series of passenger-carrying aircraft which culminated in the DC-3, the most famous of all airliners for the next two decades. The company made military aircraft, too, but most were troop carriers and not many carried weapons; only two torpedo bombers, one of them carrier-based, a dive bomber and a couple of medium bombers entered service during the prewar period.

All that changed as tensions built up towards World War 2. In response to a 1938 US Army Air Corps attack specification, Jack Northrop and Ed Heinemann came up with a twin-engine two-seat fighter, intruder and three-seat bomber, and the DB-7 series was developed into one of the more important combat aircraft, the A-20 Boston and Havoc. Sporting the first nosewheel undercarriage seen in a

military aircraft, it was an altogether modern type, much faster and more complex than its European contemporaries. The first DB-7s entered service with the French Armée de l'Air in May 1940, just in time for the fall of France, but some escaped to Britain where they were joined by others ordered for the RAF.

Ed Heinemann and Robert Donovan prepared the design of the A-26 Invader as a natural successor to the DB-7 family, using the powerful new R-2800 engine from Pratt & Whitney. Larger than its predecessor and intended from the outset for use as an attack bomber, it was the first such aircraft to use a laminar-flow wing, double-slotted flaps and remote-control turrets. It was also some 700 pounds lighter than originally estimated and could carry twice the specified bomb load, and at more than 350 mph was faster than any other bomber with the exception of the Mosquito.

The Invader's armament was comprehensive. The internal bomb load of 4000 pounds was later supplemented by 2000 pounds under the wings, and the dorsal and ventral turrets each wielded two 0.5 inch Browning machine guns in addition to the six guns fixed in the nose. Other versions had cannon in the nose and the A-26C had a glazed nose, with two 0.5 inch guns, for visual bombing and acting as lead ship with formations of solid-nosed A-26Bs.

Work was under way in 1943 on a two-seat night fighter version with radar in the nose, four 20 mm cannon in a ventral tray and a proposed dorsal turret with four machine guns. But its performance was no better than that of the Northrop P-61A Black Widow which was already in production, so development of the night fighting variant was dropped.

About 2500 A-26s were delivered, and the type had the lowest loss rate of any bomber in the European theatre. Still in service in 1948 when the B-26 Marauder was withdrawn from service, the Invader was redesignated B-26 – which led to some confusion – and carried on for many years.

As World War 2 ended and military aircraft

production abruptly ceased, the Invader design and development team at Douglas was dispersed, but the bomber was far from retirement. It proved useful in Korea and again in Vietnam, to the point where it was being manufactured urgently once again in 1963 as the B-26K, and rebuilt as the A-26A. The new model had wingtip tanks, another 500 hp per side and carried a total of 8000 pounds of bombs, internally and on eight outer-wing pylons. While it lacked the defensive turrets, it sprouted six machine guns in the wings, with eight guns or four 20 mm cannon in the nose.

The B-26K Invader acquitted itself well in Vietnam, being a popular aircraft for night attacks on the Ho Chi Minh Trail and other interdiction targets. Top speed was reduced to 350 mph, but it could deliver its comprehensive armament accurately over a wide radius, and the Douglas attack bomber had a combat career longer than almost any other type.

Art McKinley flies the Collings Foundation's A-26 *Mighty Mouse* out of Houston, Texas. *Philip Makanna*

• Douglas A-26 Invader		
Manufacturer:	........Douglas Aircraft Company	
Type:	......................Three-seat attack bomber	
Engines:	.................Two Pratt & Whitney R-2800-27 Double Wasp 18-cylinder radial, air cooled, 2000 hp	
Wingspan:	..............70 ft	.......................21.34 m
Length:	...................50 ft	.......................15.24 m
Height:	...................18 ft 6 in	.................5.64 m
Empty weight:	........22,370 lb	.................10,145 kg
Max loaded:	...........32,000 lb	.................14,515 kg
Max range:	............1400 miles	..............2253 km
Max speed:	............355 mph	................571 km/h
First flight:	..............10 July 1942	
In production:	.........1943-1946 (see text)	

ENGLISH ELECTRIC CANBERRA

WD955, a Canberra T.17A, was built at Preston in 1951 as a Canberra B2. In April 1960 it was transferred to 245 Squadron RAF Signals Command to begin its association with the secretive world of electronic warfare. Conversion to T.17 standard was started at Samlesbury during1966 and the aircraft joined No 360 Squadron at RAF Cottesmore in May 1970. The squadron moved to Wyton in 1975.

WD955 returned to Samlesbury in 1985 for upgrade to T.17A standard which included increased generating power to cope with an increase in EW equipment, necessitating an increase in the number of aerials under the wings. *Gordon Bain*

Not many air forces would give much publicity to the fact that one of their front-line aircraft, not a historic museum piece to be brought out on special occasions but a real operational type, was more than 40 years old. Towards the end of 1995 the RAF retired some of its older Canberra bombers with the disbandment of No 360 Squadron at RAF Wyton, Cambridgeshire. The oldest of them all, WD955, was made in 1951 and senior to any of its pilots.

But its longevity is a credit to the original designers of the Canberra, as well as those in the Air Staff who drew up the original specifications. Such has been the versatility of Britain's leading light jet-powered bomber over the years that when the new NATO aircraft was designated MRCA (multi-role combat aircraft) some time ago, it was said only half-jokingly that it stood for Must Refurbish Canberra Again!

World War 2 was only just over when Specification B.3/45 was issued for a medium bomber. Unarmed like the original Mosquito it was to replace, by virtue of its altitude and speed (specified as 50,000 feet and "as high as possible" but not less than 440 knots at 40,000 feet), it would be powered by two of the new Rolls-Royce axial-flow Avon engines and carry a crew of two, with bomb aiming by radar for accuracy.

A contract was signed in January 1946 for four prototype English Electric AI aircraft, and design went ahead under W.E.W. Petter. Much funding went towards specialised equipment and testing facilities, especially wind tunnels which proved to be a wise investment for future designs as well. The original intention was to have the engines half-buried in the wing roots, similar to the Comet airliner's arrangement, but problems with the Avon engine led to a re-design to take centrifugal-flow Nenes which needed to be mounted on the wings. Rolls-Royce designers believed that the axial-flow compressor would be smaller and lighter than the centrifugal version, as well as giving a lower specific fuel consumption with its greater efficiency. Time has proved them right as all major jet engines have the straight-through layout, and improved Avons were ready in time for the new bomber's test flying programme.

The radar bombing system fell behind schedule and the designers reverted to a visual bombing system, with a clear nose and a third crew member. Cramped quarters were always a complaint of the type – excessive heat under the 'greenhouse' one-piece canopy was another – but finally the new bomber was ready to fly. Wing Commander Roland Beamont took off in the first prototype in the early morning of Friday 13 May 1949 to usher in a new era of military aircraft. He demonstrated it at Farnborough that September with a spectacular show of high and low speed handling, plus rolls and other manoeuvres more appropriate to a fighter than a bomber.

Only later was it named the Canberra after the

• English Electric Canberra B.Mk 2		
Manufacturer:	........English Electric Ltd	
Type:	......................Bomber reconnaissance	
Engines:	.................Two Rolls-Royce Avon RA.3 Mk 101 axial flow turbojet, 6500 lb s.t.	
Wingspan:	.............63 ft 11 in	..............18.49 m
Length:	...................65 ft 6 in	................19.96 m
Height:	..................15 ft 7 in	................4.75 m
Empty weight:	........22,200 lb	................10,070 kg
Max loaded:	..........46,000 lb	................20,865 kg
Max range:	............2660 miles	.............4281 km
Max speed:	............570 mph	................917 km/h at 40,000 ft
First flight:	.............May 1949	

capital city of Britain's distant Dominion. That may or may not have had any bearing on the Australians' decision to manufacture 48 of them under licence at the Government Aircraft Factory, and the Canberra also became the first modern military aircraft to be made under licence in the USA. Martin built 403 as B-57s, some of which were later converted to ultra high-altitude strategic reconnaissance aircraft with 122 foot wingspans and extra engines slung underneath in pods.

Exported to many countries and in military service longer than any other postwar jet aircraft, the distinctive Canberra shape has been seen in almost all parts of the world. Many are on static display in museums, particularly in England, Australia and New Zealand, while No 39 Squadron RAF still operates PR9s on constant call for various types of work and a few are flying in private hands.

No 360 Squadron practises for its disbandment fly-past during September 1995. At the time WD955, "EM", was the oldest aircraft in active RAF service. *Gordon Bain*

Fairey Swordfish

Made by Blackburn, W5856 was originally based in Gibraltar and then went to Nova Scotia. Sir William Roberts bought it for his Strathallan collection and it later went to the Swordfish Heritage Trust for full restoration by British Aerospace, painted in the colours of Capt Nigel Skene, CO of No 810 TSR Squadron, who was awarded the DFC while flying a Swordfish off the Norwegian coast. It is flown here by Cmdr Phil Shaw RN. *Gordon Bain*

At first glance, whoever laid down the original specification which resulted in the Fairey Swordfish, let alone those who ordered it into combat against a vastly superior enemy some years later, should have been severely reprimanded at least. Anachronistic, inadequately armed, ungainly and slow, when it was first built this open-cockpit biplane harked back more than a dozen years, to the days just after World War 1 when the mark of an aeroplane's serviceability was the number of struts and wires it could present to the passing breeze. Its nickname of 'Stringbag' may have been affectionate, but it had a very real basis.

And yet this unlikely throwback proved itself to one of the better success stories of World War 2, an apparently inferior aircraft which inspired fierce loyalty among its aircrew. The British have always sided with the underdog, perhaps because their clinging to engineering and other traditions has made them underdogs themselves in so many cases, and the Swordfish was certainly underdog material. Who else but the British would expect anybody to fly an open-cockpit biplane for 10 hours on a return trip to attack an enemy warship with a torpedo?

Underdogs, perhaps, but definitely of the heroic variety. The Swordfish's superior agility allowed it to out-turn faster monoplane fighters, which could be a handy trick inside the Norwegian fjords where a pursuing Bf 109 might be enticed into a rock wall.

One Swordfish flew 12 minelaying sorties in 24 hours, and a handful based in Malta sank an average of 50,000 tonnes of enemy shipping every month in 1941-1943, most of which was heavily armed with flak. Another dropped the torpedo which crippled the steering of the battleship *Bismarck*, allowing warships of the Home Fleet to catch and later sink the pride of the German fleet. But the Swordfish highlight, for which it is best remembered, was the raid on the Italian naval base of Taranto in November 1940. In exchange for two aircraft shot down, the force of torpedo-carrying Swordfish sank three battleships, a cruiser, two destroyers and other warships, the crews of which were resting secure in harbour behind anti-torpedo nets.

There were failures, of course, the worst of which being the unsuccessful action to stop the *Scharnhorst*, *Gneisenau* and *Prinz Eugen* from breaking out from the French port of Brest in February 1942. All Swordfish were shot down, both by the naval guns and the covering Fw 190s, and only three crew members returned. Lieutenant Commander Eugene Esmonde, who led the Swordfish, was posthumously awarded the Victoria Cross.

Altogether 2391 Swordfish were delivered, 1699 of them made by Blackburn Aircraft. Fairey designed it to specification S.38/34, a two- or three-seat long-range torpedo-carrying bomber. The result flew well enough, if slowly because of all the built-in drag, on the power of its 690 hp Bristol Pegasus radial engine, while later models had a 750 hp Pegasus. It was woefully lacking in defensive armament, however. In true World War 1 style it had a single fixed 0.303 in Vickers machine gun firing through the propeller arc and a

• Fairey Swordfish	
Manufacturer:	The Fairey Aviation Company and Blackburn Aircraft
Type:	Two-seat torpedo carrier
Engine:	One Bristol Pegasus 30 9-cylinder radial, air cooled, 750 hp
Wingspan:	45 ft 6 in ....13.87 m
Length:	35 ft 8 in ....10.87 m
Height:	12 ft 4 in ....3.76 m
Empty weight:	4700 lb..................2134 kg
Max loaded:	7510 lb..................3410 kg
Max range:	546 miles................879 km
Max speed:	138 mph ....222 km/h
First flight:	17 April 1934
In production:	1935-1944

Browning or Vickers on a swivel mount for the rear gunner to face the multiple guns and cannon of pursuing Bf 109s and Fw 190s. As well as the torpedo slung under the fuselage, it could carry 1500 pounds of bombs or, in the later version with enclosed cockpit and metal-covered lower wings, eight 60 pound rockets.

At the bottom end of its performance envelope, the low stalling speed, reliable engine and ruggedness of this large fabric-covered biplane endeared it to its pilots. Nothing else could be hauled off a carrier deck at night in a blizzard – and, much more importantly, slammed back on that same pitching deck hours later, picking up the arrester wire and with the widespread fixed undercarriage being sure to take the strain.

The White Cliffs of Dover, a slow biplane which was operated with distinction right through World War 2, a White Ensign trailing in the breeze and a snappy salute from the chap in the rear cockpit – what could possibly be more British? Dave Knight is at the helm of the Royal Navy Historic Flight's Swordfish in July 1993. *Philip Makanna*

GRUMMAN TBF/TBM AVENGER

The Alpine Fighter Collection's TBM-3 is painted as *Plonky*, Fred Ladd's Avenger which he flew for 33 operational sorties in the Solomons with the RNZAF. Rex Dovey is at the controls over Lake Wanaka.
John King

Grumman was never noted for making fragile or ineffectual aircraft, particularly the military types which were its mainstay. Indeed, the company earned the affectionate sobriquet "Grumman Iron Works", appreciated by its pilots and ground crew for the strength built into its range of fighters and bombers.

The Avenger was a case in point. Under Bill Schwendler, the Grumman design team swiftly came up with the largest carrier-based single-engine aircraft on the Allied side of World War 2, with a generous size of wing, adequate power, internal weapons bay and good handling, although it tended to develop a pilot's arm muscles. Originally intended as a torpedo bomber, its usefulness later included the roles of photographic reconnaissance, conventional and dive bomber, anti-submarine strike, target towing, garden destroying and carrier on-board delivery with seven passenger seats.

Being a large (54 foot wingspan) aircraft intended from the start for carrier use, the Avenger naturally had folding wings. It carried a crew of three and, in addition to its load of one 22 inch torpedo or maximum bomb weight of 2000 pounds and underwing racks for rockets, had adequate defensive armament. A single ventral manually aimed 0.30 inch machine gun and turret 0.50 gun looked after rearward defence, while firing forward were a single fuselage mounted 0.30 inch gun plus a 0.50 inch weapon in each outer wing. Later models had no turret.

As with most wartime aircraft, production was also undertaken outside the original company's factory. Grumman built 2293 TBF Avengers and the Eastern Aircraft Division of the General Motors Corporation made 7546 TBMs, a total of almost 10,000. Production proceeded as quickly as the design, and by the time of the Battle of Midway, just over two years after the first two prototypes were ordered, large numbers were in service with the US Marine Corps and US Navy. From then on the Avenger made a significant contribution to American air power.

The Royal Navy's Fleet Air Arm also operated Avengers. In the European theatre it was credited with sinking 38 U-boats as a carrier-borne aircraft, also being used as a torpedo and conventional bomber, and during the long Pacific campaign the FAA operated it as a land-based bomber. The RNZAF flew 48 Avengers as dive bombers from jungle airfields, also in the Pacific, and in a significant secondary role sprayed diesel oil on Japanese soldiers' gardens, depriving them of food.

But more warlike were the operations from aircraft carriers, taking part in major Pacific battles which included Guadalcanal, Gilbert Islands, Marshall Islands and the Battle of the Philippines. Avengers also took part in actions which resulted in the sinking of the Japanese carriers *Ryujo*, *Hiyo*, *Chiyoda*, *Chitose*, *Zuiho* and *Zuikaku*, and late in the war contributed 10 torpedo hits to the sinking of the major Japanese battleship *Yamato*.

The Avenger's usefulness did not stop at the end of the war. Aircraft were refurbished at the factory until August 1954 and they stayed in service with US forces until the advent of the Douglas Skyraider. As

• Grumman TBF-1C Avenger		
Manufacturer:	........Grumman Aircraft Engineering Corporation	
Type:	......................Carrier-based torpedo/attack bomber	
Engine:	..................One Wright Double Cyclone R-2600-8 18-cylinder radial, air cooled, 1700 hp	
Wingspan:	..............54 ft 2 in	................16.15 m
Length:	..................40 ft	................12.19 m
Height:	..................16 ft 5 in	................5.0 m
Empty weight:	........10,555 lb	................4788 kg
Max loaded:	..........17,364 lb	................7876 kg
Max range:	............2355 miles	............3757 km
Max speed:	............242 mph	................389 km/h at sea level
First flight:	..............1 August 1941	
In production:	1942-1945	

well as New Zealand, where they stayed in regular use until 1959, mostly as target tugs, Avengers were also operated by armed services in Canada, The Netherlands, Uruguay, France and Japan.

Even in retirement they soldiered on in a swords-to-ploughshares role. The RNZAF used one for aerial topdressing trials in 1948, but usefulness kept them going in greater numbers than most other warbirds. The Avenger's weight-carrying capability and agility, despite its size, lent itself to water bombing forest fires in the American northwest right into the present era.

Today they are valued for their warbirds role, as fine aircraft finally retired to a private role, impressing airshow spectators as a noisy and big but agile performer with many more moving airframe parts than can be found in any mundane fighter.

Kermit Weeks bases this TBM with his Florida aviation collection, and flies it here just off the coast near Miami. *Philip Makanna*

HAWKER HIND

Philip Makanna

· **Hawker Hind Mk 1**

Manufacturer:	........Hawker Aircraft Ltd	
Type:	......................Light bomber	
Engine:	...................One Rolls-Royce Kestrel V V-12 cylinder, liquid cooled, 640 hp	
Wingspan:	..............37 ft 3 in	................11.35 m
Length:	...................29 ft 7 in	................9.02 m
Height:	...................10 ft 7 in	................3.23 m
Max weight:	..........5298 lb	....................2402 kg
Max range:	.............430 miles	...............692 km
Max speed:	.............186 mph	.................299 km/h
First flight:	.............12 September 1934	
In production:	1935-1938	

Although it went unrecognised at the time and became apparent only with the benefit of hindsight, British military aviation of the late 1920s and into the 1930s had a problem. It was a problem that many other nations would dearly have loved to need to cope with, but it was a problem nevertheless. Quite simply, Britain had a range of military aircraft which was too good.

It was all due to Sydney (later Sir Sydney) Camm, chief designer for Hawker Engineering, which was reorganised in 1933 into Hawker Aircraft. Back in 1928 he came up with the Hart, a light two-seat bomber which, although it differed little from World War 1 technology in being a fabric-covered biplane, had a metal structure and sleek lines. The Air Ministry had been embarrassed by the speed of the 1918 DH4 bomber, which could outrun most of its contemporary fighters. Seven years later the Fairey Fox did the same, which led to some official re-thinking and a call for a light day bomber very different from the lumbering giants which had evolved. Avro, Fairey and Hawker all vied for the contract, and the result was the Hart which spawned a dozen or so variants, all looking similar but differing in specifications and purpose.

The Hart was developed in conjunction with Rolls-Royce, which was working on the F.XI, a new version of the liquid cooled V-12 Falcon with weight-saving cylinder blocks in place of individual cylinders. Renamed the Kestrel and later producing more than 600 hp in supercharged form, it paved the way for the Schneider Trophy-winning R-type and, more important historically, the Battle of Britain-winning Merlin.

The Kestrel's low frontal area allowed a sleek nose, and Camm's Hart was a notably elegant two-seat biplane of unequal span and with the top wings swept back. Its performance and other advantages led to a policy of almost a single-type air force, which ironically retarded aircraft development in much the same way as the Polikarpov I-16's dominance prevented Soviet advances in fighter design.

From the two-place Hart came the Hardy two-seat general purpose aircraft and Demon two-seat fighter of 1932, as well as the Hartbees, 65 of which were made under licence in Pretoria for the SAAF. The 1930 Osprey was a shipboard Hart with folding wings, naval equipment and strong points for catapult launching, still powered by Kestrel, while the Nohab was an Osprey with a Mercury radial engine for the Swedish Navy. The 1932 Audax was made for army cooperation with a message hook and other equipment, and led to the Hector five years later, with 805 hp Napier Dagger H-24 engine and straight top wings.

The ultimate in British single-seat biplane fighters was the Fury of 1932, fast at 200 mph and most elegant, and exported with a bewildering variety of engines, both in-line and radial. That led to the Kestrel-engined Nimrod for the FAA, and the last in the Hart-inspired line was the single-seat PV3 fighter with 695 hp steam-cooled Rolls-Royce Goshawk engine, but that was not proceeded with. The engine cooling had problems and changes in RAF fighter requirements led to work on the Hurricane, which was originally conceived as a Hawker private venture, a Fury monoplane.

Also dating from 1934 was the Hawker Hind, another light bomber development of the Hart. Altogether 528 Hinds were made, although the change to more modern monoplane bombers led to a number of the final Hinds being converted on the production line to dual-control trainers. Many were exported, notably to Latvia, Persia, South Africa and New Zealand, the RNZAF receiving 63 Hinds from September 1940 as bombers, army cooperation aircraft and pilot trainers, the promised AT-6 Harvards still being some way off.

Surplus and obsolete military aircraft are seldom preserved, alas, and very few of the more than 3500 Hart/Demon/Fury/Hind/etc variants built have been kept in any form, let alone as active warbirds. A replica Fury has been flown in England, however, and with an airworthy Hind and one or two long-term rebuild projects, the world will continue to be reminded of Sydney Camm's elegant biplane fighter-bomber creation.

Hawker's related series of fighters and light bombers marked the epitome of the classic 1930s fighting biplane. Dodge Bailey flies the Shuttleworth Collection's Hind near Duxford, England.
Philip Makanna

MARTIN B-26 MARAUDER

Philip Makanna

With a long record of bombers as well as civil flying boats to its credit, Martin made a big effort to win the USAAC's just-prewar medium bomber competition. Issued in January 1939, the specification called for a heavily armed medium bomber, fast at 350 mph and with a range of more than 2000 miles, a service ceiling of 20,000 feet and a heavy bomb load.

What the specification failed to mention were take-off and landing speeds, an unusual omission. But that gave the designers an opportunity to use a small wing area with high loading to optimise cruise speed, and Peyton M. Magruder combined that feature with a circular cross-section fuselage, of constantly changing diameter and with the minimum number of excrescences, to give low drag and good capacity. His design proposal won the company approval of Glenn Martin himself, and on 5 July the Martin Model 179 was submitted to the USAAC. Included in the proposal was the use of the new Pratt & Whitney R-2800 Double Wasp engines, along with guaranteed performance and a production schedule promising quick delivery.

Such factors were highly important in the tense period of rearmament leading up to World War 2, and the Model 179 gained a clear lead over its rivals. Winning the contest brought a production contract for the unprecedented total of 1100 units and the

new Martin bomber was the first American aircraft to be ordered off the drawing board, although the practice was by no means unusual later in the war.

The first flight took place just over a year later, and three months after that the first production examples began leaving the line at Baltimore, Maryland. They were deployed to Australia the day after the bombing of Pearl Harbor brought the USA into the war, and by April 1942 some 48 B-26As were based in northern Australia, from where they bombed Rabaul by means of refuelling at Port Moresby and having a fuel tank in the rear bomb bay which limited their bomb load to 2000 pounds. They were also used as torpedo strike aircraft in the Battle of Midway and in the Aleutian Islands, and in the Middle East and Western Desert as tactical bombers.

But the introduction of the B-26 was not without its problems. The popular press of the day dubbed it the 'Flying Torpedo', but it earned a nasty reputation as the 'Flying Prostitute' and 'Widow Maker' with its record for training accidents. No fewer than four investigation boards were formed to discuss its future production and development, usually resulting in temporary suspension of production and finally in the recommendation to incorporate several changes, including an increase in wing area. Perseverance, and doubtless better training, finally resulted in the B-26 setting the record for the lowest loss rate of any USAAF bomber in Europe, less than one-half of one percent in tactical operations against heavily defended French and German targets.

The larger wing was offset by official calls for still-heavier loads, and the resulting slightly lower speed was not helped by external armament which spoiled the B-26's aerodynamic perfection. B-26B-10s, sprouting no fewer than twelve 0.5 inch machine guns, were useful at the end of the Tunisian campaign when they intercepted German transports well out over the Mediterranean Sea, shooting them down as they evacuated the beaten German forces.

• Martin 179 B-26G Marauder	
Manufacturer:	The Glenn L. Martin Company
Type:	Medium bomber
Engines:	Two Pratt & Whitney R-2800-43 Double Wasp 18-cylinder radial, air cooled, 2000 hp
Wingspan:	71 ft ... 21.64 m
Length:	56 ft 6 in ... 17.23 m
Height:	21 ft 6 in ... 6.55 m
Empty weight:	25,300 lb ... 10,433 kg
Max loaded:	38,200 lb ... 17,340 kg
Max range:	1150 miles ... 1850 km
Max speed:	280 mph ... 451 km/h
First flight:	25 November 1940
In production:	1941-1945

More than 5000 Martin Marauders were made, and all remaining aircraft were withdrawn from service in 1948 with the B-26 designation passing to the Douglas Invader. Despite its early reputation and landing speed of 130 mph which stayed unchanged despite the modifications, the Marauder was a useful bomber with no flying characteristics which really could be termed vicious. Single-engine performance was good, but it did call for a high standard of training, and with a good pilot it gave a good account of itself in many theatres of World War 2.

The B-26's wide fuselage of circular cross section and shoulder wings give it a pugnacious air. Tony Ritzman flies Kermit Weeks's Marauder near Chino, California. *Philip Makanna*

NORTH AMERICAN B-25 MITCHELL

Executive Sweet is a B-25J built in 1944 and is now based at Camarillo, California, where it is owned by the AAF Museum. It was flown by Jeff Kertes for this photo sortie on 27 May 1994 on a flight out of Watsonville, California. *Gordon Bain*

Combat aircraft are not usually named after people, but one exception bore a singularly apt title. William "Billy" Mitchell was a feisty US Army Air Corps colonel whose belief in air power perhaps stemmed from his being the first US Army officer to fly over the German lines in 1917. His persistence and outspokenness led to his court martial in 1925 – and posthumous promotion to the rank of brigadier-general, 10 years after his death in 1936.

Mitchell, the aircraft, came from a company with no previous experience in twins, bombers or high-performance warplanes of any sort, but it has been described as the best in the medium bomber class in World War 2 and was made in larger quantities, almost 10,000, than any other American twin-engine combat aircraft.

North American's design team, under Lee Attwood and Ray Rice, came up with the NA-40 in response to the 1938 US Army specification 98-102 for a twin-engine medium bomber. Of somewhat stubby outline with tricycle undercarriage, it carried a 1200 pound bomb load on the power of its Pratt & Whitney Twin Wasp radial engines. Before it could

see much production or development, however, the specifications changed to double the bomb load and an extensive redesign resulted in the NA-62, retaining the general layout with shoulder wing and twin tails but rather sleeker in appearance. Engines were Wright Double Cyclones of 1350 hp each.

The US Army ordered 184 B-25s off the drawing board in September 1939, and less than a year later the first example was flown. Following the first two dozen B-25s, the B-25A was given self-sealing fuel tanks and armour protection for the crew, in response to air combat reports from Europe, and the bomb load was raised to 3000 pounds.

Defensive armament varied according to model, but typically comprised dorsal and ventral turrets, two forward firing 0.5 inch guns in the glazed nose and one in the tail. The B-25H had a solid nose packing a 75 mm cannon and eight 0.5 inch machine guns, plus two in waist bulges and two each in dorsal and tail turrets, but most Mitchell bombers, 4318 of them, were B-25Js. They normally carried a 3000 pound bomb load, or 4000 pounds on short missions, had a glazed nose for the bomb aimer and bristled with 0.5 inch guns, 13 of them, while the attack version had an extra five machine guns in the solid nose.

Ventral turrets were removed from 16 B-25Bs in favour of extra fuel load for one of the most audacious raids of World War 2 – the attack on Tokyo and other Japanese mainland targets in April 1942. Led by Lt Col James H. Doolittle, they took off from the deck of the carrier USS *Hornet*, where they had been lashed down as they were too big to be stowed below in the hangar, some 800 miles from the Japanese capital. The distance was further than planned, because of an encounter with a Japanese patrol boat, and after successfully bombing Tokyo, Kobe, Yokohama and Nagoya all 16 aircraft were lost through bad weather and shortage of fuel when trying to land at their intended terminal bases in China.

But most of the crews survived and the attack was

• North American B-25J Mitchell	
Manufacturer:	........North American Aviation Inc.
Type:	......................Medium bomber
Engines:	................Two Wright Double Cyclone R-2600-29 14-cylinder radial, air cooled, 1850 hp
Wingspan:	..............67 ft 6 in ....20.42 m
Length:	...................52 ft 11 in ....16.12 m
Height:	...................15 ft 9 in ....4.8 m
Empty weight:	........21,100 lb................9571 kg
Max overload:	........41,800 lb................18,956 kg
Max range:	............1500 miles................2414 km
Max speed:	............275 mph ....442 km/h at 15,000 ft
First flight:	..............19 August 1940
In production:	1940-1945

an enormous success, not for tactical reasons as the damage was minimal but to raise American morale after the Pearl Harbor debacle and subsequent reverses in the Pacific. The reminder to Japan of its vulnerability to air attack kept some fighter groups on home defence when they were most needed in the Solomons.

B-25s were used by many Allied air forces in all theatres and every major battlefront of World War 2, perhaps best remembered in the Mediterranean for its starring role in Joseph Heller's classic 1961 novel *Catch-22* and the film of the book some years later. The Mitchell bomber was retained by many air forces well into the postwar era, and its peaceful roles include carrying Cinerama cameras. Today nothing can surpass the B-25 as a camera platform for warbird photography, with a clear view from the aft-facing seat where the tail turret used to be.

Show Me! is a B-25J Mitchell now part of the Confederate Air Force, photographed out of Harlingen, Texas, in 1990. *Philip Makanna*

SHORT S.25 SUNDERLAND

Sunderland NZ4115, shown at rest near its base at Hobsonville, Auckland, is now on static display on dry land at the Museum of Transport and Technology. *Charles Darby*

The respected aircraft manufacturing firm of Short Brothers was founded by Horace, Eustace and Oswald Short in 1911. It specialised in marine aircraft and did more for development of early naval flying than any other British company. The Short 184 was the first seaplane used in a naval engagement, as a spotter in the Battle of Jutland, and was also the first aircraft to sink a ship with a torpedo.

After World War 1 the company established airship works and also developed all-metal aircraft, but it was best known for its range of flying boats. Throughout the 1920s and into the following decade those grew in size as stately multi-engine biplanes, both military and civil, culminating in the Singapore flying boat with its four 560 hp Rolls-Royce Kestrel engines mounted in tandem pairs between the wings. The last Singapores, relics of the mid-1920s, were operated by the RNZAF at Suva, Fiji, on long-range search and convoy escort duties as late as April 1943.

But in 1935 Short Bros produced a flying boat design which rendered everything else obsolete. The S.23 Empire was built in response to the British Government's decision to carry all mail within the British Empire at ordinary surface rates, leading to a sudden expansion of Imperial Airways and a need for new aircraft, specifically flying boats which were

not constrained by the small and undeveloped airfields found along the mail routes.

The S.23 differed from all previous Short flying boats in being a high-wing monoplane, with streamlined nose and a deep hull which kept the four engines and propellers clear of spray. The hull depth allowed spacious cabins on two levels, and the aerodynamic efficiency with its lack of struts set a new trend in international flying boat design, most subsequent types sharing a similar layout.

A derivative of the Empire class boat was the military Sunderland, built to meet Specification R.2/33 and benefiting from the extensive aerodynamic and hydrodynamic research of the long Short flying boat development. First flown in October 1937, the Sunderland was at the time one of the heaviest aircraft in service and could lift nearly its empty weight of 27,190 pounds.

Some 740 were made, powered by either Bristol Pegasus or Pratt & Whitney Twin Wasp radial engines, and they spent their war years finding and sinking U-boats and rescuing seamen and airmen from wrecks. Defensive armament of nose, dorsal and tail turrets, plus guns fired from waist hatches, made the Sunderland anything but a sitting duck, and many times a lone flying boat managed to fight off half-a-dozen attacking aircraft, staying low over the sea to protect its vulnerable under surfaces and leaving no blind spots. Most of the crew occupied stations on the upper deck, and stores in the form of depth charges and bombs totalling 2000 pounds were stowed inboard, to be winched out on tracks under the inner wings at the appropriate time.

They were also used as transports and for evacuation of trouble spots, for example at Crete where one Sunderland was loaded until it began shipping water through one of its hatches and was found to be carrying almost 90 passengers scattered though its cavernous hull. Later transport roles included the postwar Berlin Airlift, where they landed on the lakes in the

besieged German capital, and supporting the North Greenland Expedition. Sunderlands were also used in anger in Korea and against terrorists in Malaya, but gradually their uses became more peaceful.

The last military Sunderlands were used by the RNZAF until 1967 on maritime patrol duties around the South Pacific Ocean, also providing valuable transport to remote islands. Others were converted to civil use, but a large flying boat is very expensive to maintain and their numbers have gradually diminished.

Currently the only flying example of its type, this Short Sunderland MR5 is now based in Florida as part of Kermit Weeks's collection. As ML814 it served with three squadrons based in the British Isles during World War 2 – Nos 201 RAF, 422 (Canadian) and 330 (Norwegian) – before being refurbished as part of the RNZAF re-equipment programme in 1952, when it became NZ4108 with No 5 Squadron. Sold in 1963 to Airlines of New South Wales, it later went to England and is seen here over the Solent. *Gordon Bain*

Short Sunderland Mk V	
Manufacturer:	Short & Harland Ltd
Type:	Anti-submarine/maritime patrol flying boat
Engines:	Four Pratt & Whitney R-1830-90B Twin Wasp 14-cylinder radial, air cooled, 1200 hp
Wingspan:	112 ft 9½ in ....34.39 m
Length:	85 ft 4 in ....26 m
Height:	32 ft 10½ in ....10.1 m
Empty weight:	37,000 lb ....16783 kg
Max loaded:	60,000 lb ....27,250 kg
Max range:	2690 miles..............4300 km
Max speed:	213 mph ....343 km/h at 5,000 ft
First flight:	16 October 1937
In production:	1938-1946

CAC CA-19 Boomerang

The flame-suppressing "hedgehog" exhaust pipe for the Pratt & Whitney Twin Wasp is a distinctive feature of the Boomerang. *John King*

At the start of the Pacific War in December 1941 following the attack on Pearl Harbor, the speed of the Japanese advance southwards through Malaya and the chains of islands took the Allies by surprise. Australia, a large open country with a vast and remote coastline, was difficult to defend and suddenly vulnerable. Air power had been shown to be important, but Australia's prewar air force had been reduced to a series of multipurpose aircraft and lacked serious frontline types. Even as late as September 1939 the RAAF relied on the two-seat Hawker Demon biplane as its main fighter.

No immediate assistance was forthcoming from either Britain or the USA, both of whose fighter production facilities were already fully committed, so the political decision was made for the Commonwealth Aircraft Corporation to design and build a fighter as quickly as possible to help defend Australia. Lawrence (later Sir Lawrence) Wackett led a team which began detailed design in December 1941. The Australian War Cabinet ordered 105 aircraft straight off the drawing board on 21 December and the first production Boomerang – no prototype as such was ever made – was test flown by Ken Fruin on 29 May 1942. A remarkable achievement.

To speed development, as much of the structure as possible was based on the Wirraway, an armed two-seat trainer developed by CAC from North American Aviation's NA-33, a derivative of the AT-6 Texan or Harvard. The Boomerang's all-metal wing had a strengthened Wirraway centre section and single-spar outer panels with leading-edge taper. The fuselage, of welded chrome-molybdenum steel tube in four sections bolted together, had an aluminium monocoque bottom and plywood covering of the rear fuselage. Engine choice was the 1200 hp Pratt & Whitney R-1830 Twin Wasp, already in local production under licence for the Bristol Beaufort light bomber programme.

The Boomerang was a tubby little fighter, heavier than but similar in size and speed to the much-maligned Brewster Buffalo. At a whisker over 300 mph its top speed was disappointing, but its climb rate was exceptional and mock combat exercises against the Curtiss P-40E Kittyhawk and Bell P-39 Airacobra showed the Boomerang was more manoeuvrable and a better combat aircraft, although it could never hold its own against the Japanese fighters.

Of the 250 Boomerangs made, some went to equip Nos 83 and 85 Squadrons RAAF for home defence duties and were based on Australian soil. The type's most famous role, however, was that of army support, where its rugged build and agility at low levels, combined with the fire power of its two 20 mm cannon and four 0.303 inch machine guns, made it an excellent ground attack aircraft in New Guinea and the Pacific Islands. The courage of the Boomerang pilots, as they flew at minimum altitude into solid anti-aircraft and small arms fire while locating and marking enemy positions with smoke bombs, drew unstinting praise from the Australian, New Zealand and American troops with whom they operated.

At war's end the availability of so many fighter types with better performance, quite apart from the lack of need for so many combat aircraft, made the surviving 132 Boomerangs immediately redundant.

CAC CA-19 Boomerang		
Manufacturer:	........Commonwealth Aircraft Corporation	
Type:	......................Single-seat fighter-bomber	
Engine:	....................One Pratt & Whitney R-1830 S3C4G Twin Wasp 14-cylinder radial, air cooled, 1200 hp	
Wingspan:	.............36 ft	........................10.97 m
Length:	....................26 ft 9 in	................8.15 m
Height:	....................12 ft 4 in	...............3.75 m
Empty weight:	........5373 lb	....................2437 kg
Max loaded:	..........7699 lb	....................3492 kg
Normal range:	........930 miles	...............1496 km
Max range:	.............1600 miles	............2575 km
Max speed:	............305 mph	.................491 km/h at 15,500 ft
First flight:	..............29 May 1942	
In production:	1942-1944	

Many were scrapped where they last landed on far northern airstrips, while others were reduced to components at various sites around Australia.

One of those military airfields was Oakey, on the Darling Downs in south-eastern Queensland. Parts disappeared into the surrounding farmland, but a mostly complete airframe ended up in the Darling Downs Aviation Museum, from where it was acquired by Guido and Lynette Zuccoli as the basis of Australia's first airworthy Boomerang restoration. It first flew in October 1992, 46 years after the final flight of any of the RAAF examples.

Wayne Milburn flies the Zuccoli collection's Boomerang over the Darling Downs near its base at Toowoomba, Queensland. So far the only airworthy example, it will soon be joined by others. *John King*

CHANCE VOUGHT F4U CORSAIR

A Corsair is ready for takeoff from the deck of USS Midway in April 1949. *Parker Mudge*

The Corsair, one of World War 2's outstanding combat aircraft, was mostly used in a role rather different from that originally specified, being designed as a carrier-borne fighter but seeing much of its service as a land-based fighter-bomber with a number of air arms. More than 12,500 examples were made during its 10-year production run which carried it well into the era of the jet fighter, with Corsairs seeing action with the French navy in Indochina and the 1956 Suez crisis and, even as late as 1969, in a local Central American conflict.

Development started in 1938 with a US Navy request for proposals for a single-seat carrier-based fighter. Led by Tex Beisel, the Vought design team came up with what it considered to be the smallest airframe to fit the most powerful engine available, the 2000 hp Pratt & Whitney XR-2800 Double Wasp. The new Corsair – the name had applied to a number of the company's previous products – was larger than most of its British contemporaries, particularly in height, but at the time the British had no 2000 hp engine. The relative simplicity and reliability of the American 18-cylinder radial engine kept them at the forefront of the larger and more powerful fighter design.

A large-diameter propeller was needed to take advantage of all that power, so to keep the main undercarriage legs to a practical length for rigorous carrier use and still give adequate clearance, the folding wings were given the inverted gull wing shape which made the Corsair unique. At the same time the right-angle junction of wing root and fuselage gave minimum interference drag without the need for bulky fairings, and with its power and aerodynamic efficiency the prototype Corsair became the first American fighter to exceed 400 mph in level flight, in October 1940.

But it took some time and a number of modifications for the Corsair to be accepted for carrier use, and the US Marine Corps took the first squadron into action, based in Guadalcanal in February 1943, when air supremacy over the Japanese really started. The Royal Navy's Fleet Air Arm made the first operational carrier use of Corsairs from HMS *Victorious* two months later, a year ahead of the US Navy's final acceptance of the type for deck landings after changes to the cockpit to improve pilot visibility.

Production aircraft came from Goodyear and Brewster as well as the parent company, and most Corsairs, including the Fleet Air Arm's nearly 2000 examples, saw service in the Pacific where they were more than a match for Japanese fighters. The RNZAF operated 424 Corsairs in the Solomons from 1944, making it by far the most numerous of that force's aircraft types, and one squadron went to Japan in 1946 as part of the Commonwealth Occupation Forces. The US Marines flew F4Us in the Korean War and the Aéronavale (the French naval air arm) during its own conflicts in Indochina.

The last operational Corsairs were used in the 'Soccer War' between El Salvador and Honduras in July 1969, by which time the type was already starting to be restored to flying condition by private collectors. Today it is one of the most valued of all warbirds, active in several countries.

• Chance Vought F4U-1D Corsair		
Manufacturer:	........United Aircraft Corporation	
Type:	......................Single-seat carrier-based fighter/fighter-bomber	
Engine:	...................One Pratt & Whitney R-2800-8W Double Wasp 18-cylinder radial, air cooled, 2250 hp	
Wingspan:	..............41 ft	...........................12.47 m
Length:	...................33 ft 4½ in	..............10.16 m
Height:	...................15 ft 1 in	.................4.60 m
Empty weight:	........8694 lb	...................3944 kg
Max loaded:	..........13,120 lb	.................5951 kg
Normal range:	........1015 miles	............1633 km
Max range:	............1562 miles	..............2514 km
Max speed:		
– sea level	................328 mph	.................528 km/h
– 20,000 ft	................425 mph	.........684 km/h
First flight:	..............29 May 1940	
In production:	1942-1952	

Only one ex-RNZAF Corsair is currently airworthy, with The Old Flying Machine Company at Duxford, England. In New Zealand the Alpine Fighter Collection's F4U-1 is a rare early 'bird cage' model without the bubble canopy and raised pilot's seat which led to its acceptance for carrier use. Restored to flying condition in Florida by 1979 after sitting outside for many years, it was imported in 1991 and is flown here by Keith Skilling near its Wanaka base. *John King*

CURTISS P-40 WARHAWK/KITTYHAWK

Fred Sebby flies Bill Clarke's P-40. *Philip Makanna*

Its production run of 13,738 made it one of the most numerous American-built fighters and it was praised by its pilots for its strength and agility. The P-40 was a superb attack aircraft and served with distinction in all theatres of World War 2, with more supplied to Allied air forces under Lend-Lease arrangements than to the Americans themselves.

Curtiss had a long record of building single-seat fighters, starting in 1917 with triplanes and progressing from wood-and-fabric to all-metal biplanes, after 1925 mostly named as some sort of Hawk. The first low-wing monoplane fighter, the Hawk 75, was designed by Donovan R. Berlin in response to a 1934 USAAC specification for a 300 mph all-metal fighter, using expertise gained in the A-8 Shrike project of 1931. Problems with the Pratt & Whitney R-1535 and Wright XR-1670 engines led to a shortfall in performance and the new Curtiss fighter lost out to the Seversky P-35, but with a change to Pratt & Whitney R-1830 power the Model 75 was accepted as the P-36. A new and enduring line of combat aircraft was started.

The type claimed the first war victories in two separate phases of World War 2 – in France with Hawk 75C-1s which were fairly even against the Bf 109Ds, and in Hawaii where P-36As shot down two Japanese attackers during the Pearl Harbor raid. Hawks also fought on both sides, Finland using captured aircraft and the Vichy French flying against Allied forces in North Africa and Syria.

The 10th production P-36A was re-engined with a 1040 hp Allison V-1710-19 liquid cooled V-12 engine and the company-designated Hawk 81 became the XP-40. Engine and drag-reducing development took some time, but the airframe with its reassuringly strong multi-spar wings needed nothing more than the new engine installation. Two 0.303 machine guns in the top forward fuselage supplemented the four in the wings, and the P-40Bs supplied to the RAF as Tomahawks were fitted with pilot armour and fuel tank protection. Others went to Canada, Turkey, the Soviet Union, Egypt and China.

Next came the Hawk 87, or P-40D, for which Curtiss changed in 1940 to the 1150 hp Allison engine and concentrated all the guns in the wings. The British called them Kittyhawks and the Americans Warhawks, those names staying with them for the rest of the war. Further development tried more power and better altitude performance with the Packard Merlin-powered P-40F, but that was a failure and subsequent models all had Allison engines up to 1200 hp. More power was needed to maintain performance with heavier armament and equipment, but any increased margin invariably brought still more weight in fuel or disposable load. The final version, the P-40N, was made in larger numbers than any other at 5216 and a serious effort was made to reduce weight by the use of lighter components and deleting one wing tank and two of the machine guns, but most were supplied to the Allies as the Americans were flying more modern fighters.

The P-40 earned praise for being solid, workmanlike and almost viceless. The RNZAF operated 297 Kittyhawks of various models, at first for local defence but soon acquitting itself well in the Central and Northern Solomons campaigns and claiming 99 Japanese aircraft destroyed for the loss of only 20

• Curtiss P-40N-20 Kittyhawk/Warhawk	
Manufacturer:	........Curtiss-Wright Corporation
Type:	......................Single-seat fighter/fighter-bomber
Engine:	....................One Allison V-1710-99 V-12 cylinder, liquid cooled, 1200 hp
Wingspan:	..............37 ft 3½ in..............11.36 m
Length:	....................33 ft 4 in.................10.14 m
Height:	....................12 ft 4 in.................3.75 m
Empty weight:	........6700 lb..................3039 kg
Max loaded:	...........11,400 lb................5008 kg
Normal range:	........750 miles................1207 km
Max range:	.............2800 miles.............4506 km
Max speed: – 5000 ft – 15,000 ft	 ....308 mph ....496 km/h ....343 mph ....552 km/h
First flight:	..............14 October 1938
In production:	1940-1945

Kittyhawks in combat (but 152 in accidents in New Zealand and overseas).

Flt Lt Harry Wigley, acting officer commanding No 14 Squadron RNZAF, wrote a detailed official report in July 1943 at the end of the unit's first tour of duty in the Solomons. He offered some advice on fighting the main Japanese opponent, previously unfamiliar, and stated flatly that "no P-40 can dogfight a Zero". The Kittyhawk, however, accelerated rapidly in a dive and could not be caught. "The best thing to point at a Jap is the guns. If you can't do this, point only the armour plate behind the pilot."

John Lamont flies over Lake Wanaka, New Zealand, in the Alpine Fighter Collection's P-40K which was restored in the 1990s after being salvaged from its wartime resting place in the Aleutian Islands. This fighter was later damaged in a forced landing after engine seizure, but is being rebuilt to fly again.
John King

DE HAVILLAND DH100 VAMPIRE

One of the earliest operators of the Vampire was the Swiss Air Force. It was also the last operator. These two single-seaters were used for target towing – hence the colour scheme – out of Sion and photographed shortly before the Vampire was finally retired from Flugwaffe service. *Gordon Bain*

Both Britain's first operational jet aircraft had their origins towards the beginning of World War 2, but because of the long development needed with the revolutionary form of propulsion only one, the Gloster Meteor, saw wartime service. But that long gestation period had the advantage of producing good aircraft, and both the twin-engine Meteor and single-turbojet Vampire which closely followed it were used by air forces in many countries for decades after the war.

Air Ministry Specification E.6/41 called for a single-seat interceptor fighter to be powered by one of the turbojet engines then under development, and de Havilland's answer, although unconventional, had a shape dictated by the shortcomings of the turbojet. Thrust was marginal, and so to keep power losses through air friction to a minimum in the intake and tail pipes, those had to be kept as short as possible. That called for a short fuselage, so the tail was carried on twin booms and mounted high to keep it out of the jet efflux.

The air intakes were in the roots of the tapered all-metal wings which had split trailing-edge flaps, air brakes and ailerons. Booms and tail were also metal, but the fuselage was typical de Havilland as a plywood-balsa-plywood sandwich in the manner of the Mosquito, made in two halves and joined along the centre line. Its size was dictated by the diameter of the Halford-designed de Havilland Goblin 1 centrifugal-flow turbojet, aptly named with its distinctive moan and mounted in the rear fuselage behind the pilot, and the result was a compact jet fighter with the usual de Havilland excellent handling characteristics.

Work started on the design of the new jet fighter in 1941, not long after the first flight of the Mosquito, and Geoffrey de Havilland Junior took the unarmed prototype Vampire LZ548/G for its first test on 20 September 1943. That was soon followed by two more prototypes, one of which carried the definitive armament of four 20 mm cannon, and a contract for 120 Vampire F.1s, to be made by English Electric in its Preston works, was placed in May 1943. The first production aircraft was flown in April 1945 and the first batch of 40 was used mostly for evaluation and testing, including squadron use, with development in more powerful Goblin engines, cockpit pressurisation, a lower tailplane and Mosquito slipper tanks progressively being incorporated.

Although it entered service too late for World War 2, the Vampire was an important innovation in fighters and was exported to many countries in Africa, South America, Europe, Asia, the Middle East and the Pacific, as well as serving with the RAF in all its postwar theatres. The Vampire equipped more air forces of the world with their first jet fighter than any other type, and licensed production was also carried out in Australia, Switzerland and Italy, plus local assembly of components in France and India.

The first pure jet to operate from an aircraft carrier was a Vampire, aboard HMS *Ocean* on 3 December 1945, and a naval version was used mostly for training. Many land-based variants were made, including the FB Mks 5, 6 and 9 fighter-bombers which had more power and clipped and strengthened wings for carrying external stores in the form of rockets, bombs or drop tanks. Two versions with wider forward fuselage were made to seat two occupants side-by-side, one of them an interim night fighter for the RAF and the other the T.11 trainer, more than 800 of which were made and widely used.

The de Havilland design team got it right back in the early 1940s, as shown by more than 50 years of service of the Vampire in different parts of the world.

Brett Emeny bases this Ex-Swiss Air Force Vampire T.11 at New Plymouth but is flying it here near Auckland, New Zealand. *John King*

• de Havilland DH100 Vampire FB Mk 5	
Manufacturer:	The de Havilland Aircraft Company
Type:	Single-seat fighter-bomber
Engine:	One de Havilland Goblin 2 centrifugal flow turbojet, 3100 lb s.t.
Wingspan:	38 ft .... 11.58 m
Length:	30 ft 9 in .... 9.37 m
Height:	6 ft 2 in .... 1.88 m
Empty weight:	7253 lb .... 3290 kg
Max loaded:	12,360 lb .... 5606 kg
Normal range:	590 miles at sea level .... 950 km
Max range:	1145 miles at 30,000 ft .... 1843 km
Max speed: – sea level	531 mph .... 854 km/h
– 30,000 ft	505 mph .... 813 km/h
First flight:	26 September 1943
In production:	1945-1949

DE HAVILLAND DH112 VENOM

Gordon Bain

The success of de Havilland's little Vampire jet fighter inevitably led to ideas of development, particularly in terms of more power. The third production Vampire flew in May 1947 as a testbed for the new de Havilland Ghost engine which produced almost 50 per cent more thrust although it was only slightly larger than the Goblin, and development of a Ghost-engined Vampire, at first designated Mk 8, led to a new type.

The DH112 Venom shared the Vampire's twin boom layout and plywood/balsa sandwich fuselage structure, but the bigger diameter of the Ghost engine gave it a mildly portly look behind the cockpit. The major change was in the wing, slightly enlarged and thinner with a thickness/chord ratio of 10 per cent to take advantage of the extra power and speed, with wing sweepback on the leading edge also increasing the limiting Mach number. The wing shape, fences and the fixed tip tanks were recognition features of the new Venom in comparison with its predecessor.

Armament for the first RAF version, the FB Mk 1 which began service use in August 1952, comprised strong points under the wings for up to 2000 pounds of bombs or rockets as well as the four Hispano 20 mm cannon in the lower nose. Martin-Baker ejection seats were fitted later, and complaints about the roll response led to powered ailerons in the FB Mk 4 which also had flat-topped fins and rudders, provision for underwing drop tanks and an uprated Ghost

105 engine developing 5150 pounds static thrust. Exports went to Venezuela, Italy and Iraq, while the EFW consortium made 100 FB Mk 1s and 150 FB Mk 4s for the Swiss Air Force.

The Venom performed well with a top speed of just under 600 mph, and it was one of the fastest-climbing interceptors of its day, beating many later jets. The RAF flew them in the 1950s trouble spots of Cyprus and Malaya, in the latter case at low level against Communist insurgents while based at Tengah, Singapore. No. 14 Squadron RNZAF leased a number from the RAF while also based at Tengah, as it had previously done with Vampires in Cyprus.

An all-weather night fighter version of the Venom was first flown as a company-funded prototype in August 1950. With a widened and lengthened nose for radar and seating two crew side-by-side, it went through the usual developments in engine power and tail shape, with a dorsal fin extension to balance the increased nose area. Sixty-two NF Mk 51s, similar to the NF Mk 2 but powered by the Swedish-made Ghost RM 2A engine, were supplied to Sweden's Flygvapen.

With folding wings, strengthened and long-stroke undercarriage, catapult pickup points and a V-shaped arrester hook housed above the tailpipe in a fairing resembling an insect's ovipositor, the Royal Navy's Sea Venom FAW (fighter, all-weather) stemmed from the NF two-seater. It served with the Fleet Air Arm from 1954 to 1960, including the Suez Crisis and against Yemeni rebels north of Aden. The Royal Australian Navy operated 39 Sea Venoms, mostly aboard HMAS *Melbourne,* between 1955 and 1967, and the French built them under licence as the Aquilon (North Wind) with Fiat-built Ghost engines. They were used by the Aéronavale from 1955 until 1965, notably in ground attack missions in Algeria.

Including the Swiss and French licence-built examples, almost 1500 Venoms were made during the

• de Havilland DH112 Venom FB Mk 4		
Manufacturer:	.......The de Havilland Aircraft Company	
Type:	.....................Single-seat fighter-bomber	
Engine:	.................One de Havilland Ghost 105 centrifugal flow turbojet, 5150 lb s.t.	
Wingspan:	............41 ft 8 in..................	12.7 m
Length:	.................33 ft	10.06 m
Height:	...................6 ft 8 in.....................	2.03 m
Max weight:	..........15,310 lb	6945 kg
Max range:	...........1075 miles	1730 km
Max speed: – sea level – 30,000 ft	.............597 mph.................. ....557 mph..................	961 km/h 896 km/h
First flight:	.............2 September 1949	
In production:	1950-1956	

1950s and a few are still flying today. Most of those are ex-Swiss Air Force as that organisation operated them until recently, well into the time when privately owned, retired jet warbirds were acceptable to some civil aviation authorities and able to be flown under the experimental category.

Only one later fighter, the Sea Vixen which was developed from the 1951 twin-engine supersonic DH110 prototype, came from the de Havilland stable. The company, which had its origins when Geoffrey (later Sir Geoffrey) de Havilland joined Airco in 1914 and set up under his own name after World War 1 and became one of Britain's most noted aircraft manufacturers, was absorbed into Hawker Siddeley Aviation in mid-1963 along with many other famous names.

One of the few surviving DH Venoms in flying condition, this former Swiss Air Force Venom, J-1542, was photographed over the south of England where it is based at Bournemouth Airport with Jet Heritage.
Gordon Bain

FAIREY FIREFLY

The FR Mk 4 Firefly's radiator was moved from under the nose to leading-edge extensions of the wing centre section. *Philip Makanna*

Fairey Aviation was one of Britain's oldest aircraft manufacturers, having been started during World War 1 by C.R. (later Sir Richard) Fairey and lasting through a series of 1960s mergers until liquidation in 1977. In that 60 years or so the company made many serviceable aircraft, some of them of quite astonishing ugliness yet popular with their pilots, but also including the Delta 2 which was the first to set a world speed record of over 1000 mph, with a March 1956 two-way average of 1132 mph.

Many of Fairey's 1920s products were floatplanes for naval service, along with fighters and two-seat light bombers serving with the RAF and some Commonwealth air arms. By the time the Fairey IIIF and Gordon came along their appearance was improving and the Fantôme (Féroce) was thought to be the best-looking of all biplane fighters when it appeared in 1935. The open-cockpit Swordfish and its likewise biplane but enclosed successor, the Albacore, reverted to the utility and the Barracuda, the first monoplane torpedo bomber with the FAA, was back to being just plain ugly.

But most of Fairey's products were useful, even if technology overtook the Battle light bomber and

made it highly vulnerable to enemy fighters. The Firefly was one of the company's best aircraft, a successful shipboard fighter in production for many years during a period when aviation technology was evolving most rapidly.

Fairey's first Fireflies were products of the mid-1920s, but the best-known fighter to carry the name was designed by H.E. Chaplin and his team in 1940 to meet specification N.5/40, a combination of the earlier N.8/39 and N.9/39. Its layout was similar to the company's Fulmar which was developed in 1938 with a Merlin engine to meet the Admiralty's urgent need for a two-seat carrier fighter, but the Firefly had the bigger Rolls-Royce Griffon engine. Aerodynamic improvements included folding elliptical wings carrying four cannon and patented Youngman flaps for use both at slow approach speeds and in the cruise.

The prototype Firefly flew in December 1941 with a 1730 hp Griffon, and deliveries began in March 1943. External stores up to 2000 pounds could be carried under the wings, with later models powered by the 2245 hp Griffon 74 driving a four-blade propeller and carrying 3000 pounds. They also had the chin radiator installation moved to leading-edge extensions of the centre section, along with square wingtips reducing the span, underwing pods for fuel and radar, and a dorsal fin extension.

Some Fireflies were made as unarmed trainers with a raised rear cockpit for the instructor, but the flush midships cabin behind the trailing edge generally housed the observer. It was roomy enough to contain radio and radar equipment, either AI for night fighters or ASH for surface- and underwater-vessel detection, and the Firefly filled a number of roles. Total production of all marks ran to just over 1700.

Exports went to the navies of Australia and the Netherlands as well as smaller numbers to the air forces of Ethiopia and Thailand. Because no jet aircraft had been developed for the Firefly's carrier-borne roles, especially anti-submarine, it continued to be devel-

• Fairey Firefly FR Mk 4		
Manufacturer:	........The Fairey Aviation Company	
Type:	......................Two-seat naval fighter	
Engine:	..................One Rolls-Royce Griffon 74 V-12 cylinder, liquid cooled, 2245 hp	
Wingspan:	..............41 ft 2 in	................12.55 m
Length:	..................37 ft 11 in	..............11.56 m
Height:	..................14 ft 4 in	................4.37 m
Empty weight:	........9859 lb	..................4472 kg
Max loaded:	..........13,927 lb	................6317 kg
Normal range:	........760 miles	................1722 km
Max range:	............1070 miles	............3105 km
Max speed:		
– sea level	................316 mph	................509 km/h
– 12,500 ft	................345mph	................555 km/h
First flight:	..............22 December 1941	
In production:	1942-1955	

oped after World War 2 and was operated from both British and Australian carriers during the Korean War. Many earlier models were rebuilt by the factory in the 1950s as twin-cockpit T.1s or armed T.2 trainers, and the final version was the Firefly 7 of 1953. Used mostly as an anti-submarine trainer, it carried the latest in sonobuoys and detection devices and was distinctive in appearance with its new tail unit and two-man rear cockpit while reverting to the chin radiator and full elliptical wings.

Few other piston-engine combat aircraft had such a long development period, and the Firefly is still to be seen, either as an active warbird or on static display in museums and private collections in several countries.

The Griffon-engined Firefly was in production for 14 years, a remarkable period for a World War 2 fighter. Lt Cdr John Beattie flies the Royal Navy Historic Flight's example off the south coast of England. *Philip Makanna*

FIAT G.59-4B

'Ciao bella' is Italian for 'Hello beautiful' or (this Fiat is flown by Australians) 'G'day gorgeous'. *John King*

Aircraft of the Axis countries are not well represented among warbirds. Indeed, the casual observer might be forgiven for thinking that the alliance of Germany, Italy and Japan either failed to produce many aircraft or else their materiel was inferior.

Nothing could be further from the truth. In many cases the production numbers of Axis fighting aircraft exceeded that of their equivalent Allied examples; and there was certainly nothing inferior about the great majority of Axis aircraft, many of which were well proven in combat in the Spanish Civil War while their Allied counterparts – and combat techniques – were still being developed and refined.

The real reason for their relative scarcity is the destruction of almost all the enemy aircraft, by both sides, as the Allies advanced across Europe and through the Pacific islands towards the end of the war. A few were retained, some of them for research purposes, but as the Axis air forces and naval air arms were dismantled there was no need to preserve any of their aircraft.

Except in Italy. That country capitulated early and so fared better in the immediate postwar years, to the extent of having its armed forces quickly reinstated. Production of fighter aircraft resumed in 1947 with the Fiat G.55A Centauro, based on a number of completed and partly completed G.55I airframes which had survived the war and the bombing of the factory.

The Fiat range of fighters in the late 1930s in many ways paralleled that of its main competitor, the Macchi series, in appearance and performance. They were designed by Ing Giuseppe Gabrielli, and his G.50 Freccia (Arrow) was Italy's first all-metal single-seat monoplane fighter to feature a retracting undercarriage, although its sliding canopy was unpopular with pilots and soon replaced by an open cockpit. The Fiat G.55 Centauro, which first flew in April 1942, was a cleaned-up fighter with an enclosed cockpit and powered by a 1475 hp Daimler-Benz 605A inverted V12, made under licence as the Fiat RA 1050 RC 58 Tifone, in place of the G.50's 870 hp Fiat A 74 RC 38 radial engine.

Postwar production concentrated on the G.55A single-seat fighter and the G.55B trainer, a tandem-seat version of the fighter being a common part of an Italian fighter lineup. Both models were first flown in 1946 and, supplemented by surviving wartime examples and other airframes built up from earlier components, were exported to Argentina and Egypt as well as supplying the Italian Aeronautica Militare.

But dwindling stocks of DB 605A engine spares resulted in a new model of Fiat fighter, the G.59, which used the existing G.55 wings, tail and fuselage but with a modified cockpit and engine installation. A dozen existing G.55 airframes were rebuilt to the new standard which adopted the Rolls-Royce Merlin 24 series, rated at 1610 hp for takeoff, and a two-seat G.55BM flew in early 1948, redesignated soon afterwards to the G.59 for Italian service, G.59-1A single-seat fighter and G.59-1B two-seat trainer. Gone was the long drooped nose of the G.55, replaced by a straighter and less pugnacious-looking Merlin profile.

For the extra pilot, the fuselage fuel tank was deleted and the front cockpit moved forward, with another fully equipped cockpit added behind. Almost half the G.59 production, around 150, was the two-seat version, which culminated in the -4B with twin bubble canopies but with less power in the form of the 1490 hp Merlin 500. Only five Fiat G.59s survive, one as an instructional airframe at a technical school,

• Fiat G.59-2A Centauro		
Manufacturer:	........Aeronautica d'Italia SA Fiat	
Engine:	...................One Rolls-Royce Merlin T.24-1 V-12 cylinder, liquid-cooled, 1610 hp	
Wingspan:	..............38 ft 10½ in	..........11.85 m
Length:	....................31 ft 0¾ in	..............9.47 m
Height:	...................12 ft 4 in	.................3.76 m
Empty weight:	........6041 lb	..................2740 kg
Max loaded:	...........7496 lb	...............3400 kg
Normal range:	........882 miles	................1420 km
Max speed:	.............368 mph	.................593 km/h at 18,700 ft
First flight:	1948	
In production:	1949-1953	

one in a museum in Rome, another as a gate guardian and two flying, one owned by Guiseppi Valenti in Italy and the other in Australia as part of the Zuccoli collection at Toowoomba, Queensland.

The Zuccoli G.59-4B was one of the last off the production line in 1953 and was decommissioned in 1960. It was bought by Guido Zuccoli in 1982 and restored to airworthiness as N59B at Sanders Aircraft Technologies, Chino, California, after which the owner flew it to ninth place in the Silver Unlimited class at the 1987 Reno Air Races and was awarded Judges' Choice in the warbirds section the following year at Oshkosh. He shipped it to Darwin, Australia, in October 1988 and today, appropriately registered as VH-LIX, it is a permanent part of the collection which is still growing at Toowoomba under the care of Guido's widow, Lynette.

The Italian desert colour scheme is distinctive, but does little to mask anything over the agricultural Darling Downs region of Queensland. Matt Handley flies the Zuccoli collection's Fiat G.59 near Toowoomba. *John King*

GLOSTER GLADIATOR

Most British fighters had cockpit doors for ease of access. *Philip Makanna*

Britain's ultimate biplane fighter may have looked anachronistic against its invariably monoplane opposition, but it proved anything but a pushover. It handled so well and was so universally popular with its pilots – except at high altitude where the complete lack of cockpit heating made itself felt – that squadron mess talk over a pint of beer in the late 1930s often revolved around how well the Gladiator would stand up to the new Bf 109 if and when war came. As things turned out, that wasn't as fanciful as it might have seemed.

The open-cockpit Gloster Gauntlet of the late 1920s, the successful contender for specification F.10/27, failed to meet the later specification F.7/30 because of its lack of speed and armament. The new contract favoured the new steam-cooled Rolls-Royce Goshawk engine, but long delays with the engine, and its ultimate failure, eliminated most of the contenders. Gloster, having been occupied with Gauntlet production, turned to the new fighter design in 1933 as the renowned H.P. Folland and his team believed the basic Gauntlet fuselage, with aerodynamic refinements, new wings and a more powerful Bristol Mercury engine, would meet the requirements.

The prototype SS.37 flew in September 1934 and was ordered into production as the Gladiator, a fabric-covered biplane years behind its time when all-metal and much faster monoplane fighters were being designed and tested. Power came from a Bristol Mercury IX of 840 hp and it had an enclosed cockpit, neat single-bay wings with flaps and ailerons on all four wings, and cantilever undercarriage with internally sprung wheels. Four guns met the specification, two in the forward fuselage and two under the lower wings.

More power, in the form of the 890 hp Mercury VIIIA, was given to the Gladiator II in 1938, along with desert filters, an internal battery for starting and a full blind-flying panel. The Sea Gladiator for the Fleet Air Arm, a replacement for the Hawker Nimrod, had full naval equipment including arrester hook and an inflatable dinghy carried in a fairing under the lower wing centre section. Of the 767 Gladiators made, some 30 per cent were exported to serve with the armed forces of Belgium, China, Finland, Greece, Iraq, Ireland, Latvia, Lithuania, Portugal, Norway and Sweden, plus some transferred from the RAF to Egyptian and South African air forces.

The Gladiator was at its peak of squadron deployment at the start of World War 2, equipping 29 home and 11 overseas units, and although it was obsolescent at that time it stayed in active service until early 1945 as the last biplane fighter of both the RAF and RN. Gloster subsequently made prototypes of more modern piston-engine fighters, but in effect the company went straight from the Gladiator into jets, the E.28/39 Whittle testbed airframe and the Meteor, the only British jet fighter to see World War 2 service.

In the meantime the Gladiator was seeing plenty of action, starting in 1938 with China against the Japanese invaders and also with the RAF in Palestine. Gladiators of the Auxiliary Air Force intercepted the first German bombing raid of Britain, over the Firth

of Forth in September 1939, and two AAF squadrons took their Gladiators to France, only to lose them in the invasion shortly afterwards.

Although the biplane was no real match for the enemy fighters, in the right hands it could be a formidable foe. Tales of Gladiatorial heroism reflect the British response to the underdog, such as aircraft from the torpedoed HMS *Glorious* being operated from the frozen Lake Lesjaskogsvatn in support of the Norwegian resistance to that German invasion.

But the most stirring episode occurred in June 1940. Four Sea Gladiators were assembled from crated spare airframes on Malta, and for the next three weeks they provided the beleaguered Mediterranean island's sole air defence against the attacking Regia Aeronautica. Only three were serviceable at any one time, becoming known as *Faith*, *Hope* and *Charity*. Stories of the last British biplane fighter have lasted much longer than its time in service.

Britain's last biplane fighter made a significant contribution to the war effort. Angus McVitie flies the Suttleworth Collection's Gloster Gladiator near Duxford. *Philip Makanna*

• Gloster Gladiator I	
Manufacturer:	Gloster Aircraft Company
Type:	Single-seat fighter
Engine:	One Bristol Mercury IX or IXS 9-cylinder radial, air cooled, 840 hp
Wingspan:	32 ft 3 in .... 9.85 m
Length:	27 ft 5 in .... 8.38 m
Height:	10 ft 4 in .... 3.17 m
Empty weight:	3450 lb .... 1565 kg
Max loaded:	4864 lb .... 2206 kg
Normal range:	440 miles .... 708 km
Max speed:	253 mph .... 407 km/h
First flight:	12 September 1934
In production:	1937-1940

GRUMMAN F4F WILDCAT

Dave Morss flies his California based Grumman Wildcat during May 1998. This very F4F performed the type's last aircraft carrier landing and takeoff during 1995 when it operated from the USS *Carl Vinson*. *Gordon Bain*

Grumman Aircraft Engineering Corporation was started in Farmingdale, New York, in 1929 to make shipboard aircraft for the US Navy and Coast Guard. The first to reach production was the FF-1 which flew in December 1931, an all-metal biplane two-seat fighter with retractable undercarriage which was faster than the single-seat naval fighters then in service.

Developed from the FF-1 and retaining the enclosed cockpit, landing gear manually retracting into the lower forward fuselage and generally tubby outline was the single-seat F2F-1, first delivered in January 1935 and lasting in service until 1940. Powered by a 650 hp Pratt & Whitney R-1535, it could fly at just over 200 mph, but a major redesign resulted in the F3F-1, with slightly more power and speed but aerodynamic refinements and better directional stability and manoeuvrability. More improvements and Wright Cyclone power led to the F3F-2 and -3, Grumman's last prewar biplane fighters.

The XF4F-1 was actually started as another biplane but was changed on the drawing board to a mid-wing monoplane, still bearing an obvious family resemblance to the previous Grumman products. The XF4F-2 competed for a US Navy contract with the Brewster B-239 XF2A-1, but although it was slightly faster than the Brewster it suffered in some respects and had engine teething troubles, so it lost out. Another major redesign effort gave it numerous airframe changes, most obviously longer wings and squared-off tail surfaces, plus a Pratt & Whitney XR-1830-76 with two-speed supercharger and 1200 hp for takeoff.

The resulting F4F-3 was an attractive fighter for the US Navy which signed an initial contract in August 1939, but that order was preceded by one of almost 100 for the French Marine Nationale. With the fall of France they were diverted to Britain to join the FAA's own orders and called Martlets, Britain's first monoplane carrier fighters. The FAA also took over 30 F4F-3As which had been assigned to Greece, and in 1944 renamed them all Wildcats in line with everybody else.

Production continued with Wright Cyclone engines as well as Twin Wasps, and the F4F-4 introduced folding wings, another pair of wing-mounted 0.5 in guns and underwing racks for two 250 pound bombs. With the exception of some F4F-7 photo reconnaissance versions still made by Grumman, production was transferred to the Eastern Aircraft Division of General Motors and renamed FM-1, fully three-quarters of all Wildcats being made by that company. The next model, the lightened FM-2, became the definitive Wildcat version which standardised the 1350 hp Wright Cyclone R-1820-56 engine, with four guns but redesigned and taller vertical tail surfaces. Some 4777 of the total Wildcat production of almost 8000 were FM-2s.

Wildcats were used right through the Pacific campaigns, in the Battles of the Coral Sea and Midway, and saw plenty of action in the attack on Guadalcanal. When the Japanese A6M-2 floatplane appeared in the Aleutians the US Navy was suddenly interested in a floatplane version of the F4F-3, and one example was fitted with Edo floats and the usual extra fin area to improve yaw stability. But while the floats and struts added little extra weight, the drag reduced the speed to the extent that the order for 100 float fighters was cancelled.

Although the design was relatively old and warplane technology quickly surpassed it, the Wildcat remained an effective fighter, strong and manoeuvrable although not particularly fast, and in the right hands it could just about cope with the Japanese Zero. Only 245 were in service in December 1941, but for the following two years the F4F was the main US Navy and Marine shipboard fighter. Even as the Hellcats began to replace them aboard the carriers they were operated from the new light escort carriers, and they certainly played a significant role in both the European and Pacific theatres of World War 2.

Howard Pardue flies his F4F Wildcat near Breckenridge. *Philip Makanna*

• Grumman F4F-4 Wildcat	
Manufacturer:	Grumman Aircraft Engineering Corporation
Type:	Single-seat carrier-based fighter
Engine:	One Pratt & Whitney R-1830-86 Twin Wasp 14-cylinder radial, air cooled, 1200 hp
Wingspan:	38 ft .... 11.6 m
Length:	29 ft .... 8.85 m
Height:	11 ft 4 in .... 3.44 m
Empty weight:	5895 lb .... 2674 kg
Max loaded:	8762 lb .... 3974 kg
Normal range:	830 miles .... 1335 km
Max range:	1275 miles .... 2050 km
Max speed:	
– sea level	274 mph .... 441 km/h
– 18,800 ft	320 mph .... 515 km/h
First flight:	2 September 1937
In production:	1940-1945

Grumman F6F Hellcat

This Grumman F6F is based with the Planes of Fame museum at Chino, California. Accompanying it are two of the ultimate piston-engine fighters operated postwar from aircraft carriers, the Grumman F8F Bearcat and its Hawker Sea Fury British contemporary. *Gordon Bain*

Many fighter manufacturers have had themes to their product names. Hawker had its series of strong and destructive winds, Hurricane, Tornado, Typhoon and Tempest; Curtiss found more Hawk variations than anybody knew existed but when in doubt reverted yet again to just plain Hawk; and while Gloster also played with the Hawk theme from 1921, it standardised on bird names starting with G, including the 1924 Gorcock (male red grouse), Guan and improbable sounding Gnatsnapper of 1928.

And Grumman has its carrier-borne Cats in an unbroken 60-year tradition. The company's earlier biplane fighters were dull and anonymous FF-1s and such, although the Canadians did name the Spanish Republican-ordered G-23 the Goblin. With the new monoplane F4F development in 1939, however, the Wildcat started a long line of fierce feline fighters. Hellcat, Tigercat, Bearcat (actually the lesser Panda), Panther, Cougar, Jaguar, Tiger and Tomcat – all that's missing is the Tabby.

The second Grumman monoplane shipboard fight-er, the F6F Hellcat, was conceived and produced in vast numbers in a hurry, faster than any American fight-er before or since. Although it was ordered at the end of June 1941, several months before the Pearl Harbor raid which precipitated the Americans into the war, the relentless Japanese advance down the chains of islands through the Western Pacific immediately after-wards highlighted the unprepared state of the American military. The F4F was close to the superi-or Japanese navy and army fighters only when it was flown by the best pilots, and what was needed was something with more power and speed. And at once!

At the time Grumman subscribed to the theory that power and speed equalled size and weight, although to be fair much of the weight came from armour pro-tection of vital parts, not least among them the pilot, as the air war in Europe had already shown was need-ed. Grumman made its aircraft strong, and the Hellcat was able to absorb far more punishment than the light-ly built Zero as well as out-dive it. By the end of the war the score was Hellcats 19, Zeros 1.

Designed from scratch, the Hellcat differed from its predecessor in more than just an extra four feet in span and length. The main fuel tank was beneath the cockpit and the folding wings, now low instead of mid-mounted, had backwards-retracting main gear legs, six 0.5 inch guns and attachments for six rock-ets, with centre-section pylons for 2000 pounds of bombs. The first prototype XF6F-1, powered by a 1700 hp Wright XR-2600-10 Cyclone, flew just under a year after that first order and was followed short-ly afterwards by the definitive XF6F-3 with 2000 hp of Pratt & Whitney R-2800-10 Double Wasp.

Fifteen squadrons were equipped within nine months, as series manufacture was well underway in the autumn of 1942 in a new factory still being built around the production lines. Getting the design right in the first place led to a lack of development and engineering changes and allowed no fewer than 12,272 Hellcats to be made in little over two years.

• Grumman F6F-3 Hellcat

Manufacturer:	Grumman Aircraft Engineering Corporation
Type:	Single-seat carrier-based fighter/fighter-bomber
Engine:	One Pratt & Whitney R-2800-10 Double Wasp 18-cylinder radial, air cooled, 2000 hp
Wingspan:	42 ft 10 in ....13.05 m
Length:	33 ft 7 in ....10.2 m
Height:	13 ft 1 in ....3.99 m
Empty weight:	9042 lb ....4101 kg
Max loaded:	12,186 lb ....5528 kg
Normal range:	1085 miles..............1746 km
Max range:	1620 miles..............2607 km
Max speed:	
– sea level	324 mph ....521 km/h
– 22,800 ft	376 mph ....605 km/h
First flight:	26 June 1942
In production:	1943-1945

They were assigned to the Fleet Air Arm for use in Europe and the Far East as well as the US Navy car-rier squadrons and land-based US Marines oper-ating throughout the Pacific. The few sub-types that were made included the radar-equipped F6F-5E and F6F-5N night fighters and F6F-3P and -5P for photographic reconnaissance.

After the war many went to arm other coun-tries, and the F6F's last active service was with the French at Dien Bien Phu as late as 1954. The big, beefy fighter, which did more than any other sin-gle type to win air superiority over the Japanese in the Pacific, is still to be seen in small numbers in private hands as one of the tougher warbirds.

The Lone Star Grumman F6F Hellcat is flown by Glen McDonald. *Philip Makanna*

GRUMMAN F8F BEARCAT

F8F Bearcats, and behind them F4U Corsairs and a solitary P2V Neptune, prepare to launch from the deck of USS *Midway* in April 1949. *Parker Mudge*

American fighters of the World War 2 era tended to have large and powerful radial engines, which dictated their blunt-nosed appearance, while their British counterparts used mostly in-line engines, typically the Rolls-Royce Merlin or later Griffon. The major British exception was the Hawker range of Typhoon and Tempest, powered by the Napier Sabre H-24 engine of more than 2000 hp which resulted in a blocky nose profile, but those followed the general trend of increasing size.

About mid-war, when new and faster types were being developed, the acknowledgement that engines were near their peak of reliable evolution brought about the principle of reducing airframe size and weight to gain performance. Both Hawker, with yet another fighter named the Fury, and Grumman with its Bearcat produced the ultimate in piston-engine fighters, with similar power to their predecessors but significantly less weight. And both fighters served aboard aircraft carriers well into the postwar era, as the new turbojets with their slow engine response were still an unknown quantity.

Grumman continued the Cat theme with its project G-58, designed to meet the US Navy's needs for an air superiority fighter capable of operating from the smallest carriers, and received an order in November 1943 for two XF8F-1 prototypes. Some six feet shorter in span and length than its Hellcat predecessor and with a taller fin and rudder, the Bearcat nevertheless bore a family resemblance and used the same 2100 hp Pratt & Whitney R-2800 Double Wasp radial engine. The teardrop cockpit canopy sat at the point of maximum diameter of the circular fuselage, near the wing trailing edge, with room below the cockpit floor for the main bag type fuel tank.

Unlike the Hellcat's, the wide and tall undercarriage retracted inwards. Only the wing tips folded for stowage, and an initial design feature was the provision of break points in the wings, complete with explosive bolts. The idea was that the tips would break at a known point if overstressed, and if only one broke the pilot could regain controllability by ejecting the other, long enough to bail out. The feature was abandoned later in the development programme.

First test flights confirmed the potential of the new Bearcat with a 4800 ft/min rate of climb and maximum speed of 424 mph, but it started entering operational service in May 1945, too late for World War 2. The initial contracts for 3900 F8Fs and F3Ms (Eastern Aircraft production) were cut back to a total of 1257, which operated with 24 units. Most Bearcats were F8F-1s with four 0.5 inch machine guns, but other variants included the F8F-1B with four 20 mm cannon, F8F-1N night fighter and F8F-2 with 2500 hp engine and taller fin and rudder. A few F8F-2s were made as night fighters and photo reconnaissance aircraft, and all had inner-wing racks for rockets, bombs or drop tanks.

Production ended in May 1949 and no Bearcats were in US Navy service after 1952, but that was far from the end of the type's useful operational life. Surplus aircraft were sold to the Royal Thai Air Force and the French Armée de l'Air, which gave a good account of themselves in the Indo-Chinese war between France and the communist Viet-Minh before

• Grumman F8F-1 Bearcat	
Manufacturer:	Grumman Aircraft Engineering Corporation
Type:	Single-seat carrier-based fighter/fighter-bomber
Engine:	One Pratt & Whitney R-2800-34W Double Wasp 18-cylinder radial, air cooled, 2100 hp
Wingspan:	35 ft 6 in .... 10.82 m
Length:	27 ft 8 in .... 8.43 m
Height:	13 ft 8 in .... 4.16 m
Empty weight:	7323 lb .... 3322 kg
Max loaded:	12,740 lb .... 5779 kg
Max range:	1416 miles .... 2279 km
Max speed: – 15,000 ft – 18,800 ft	423 mph .... 680 km/h 328 mph .... 605 km/h
First flight:	31 August 1944
In production:	1945-1949

28 Bearcats were passed to the (South) Vietnamese Air Force.

Although the days of F8Fs flying in anger are well past, they are still to be seen in American skies. Again like the later Hawker Furies, Bearcats are popular for competing in the annual Reno Air Races in the Unlimited class, further lightened without the military need for armour, drop tanks or other excrescences and modified to reduce drag, with the Pratt & Whitney engines having the last horsepower extracted from them.

The Bearcat is successful in racing, just as it was one of the best piston-engine fighters to serve with the US Navy. It is also one of the most spectacular warbirds currently seen in displays.

Bill Montague flies the Camarillo based F8F Bearcat for the camera during 1995. Bill is an old hand at flying the F8F – he flew them operationally when they were new! *Gordon Bain*

HAWKER HUNTER

Gordon Bain

Often described as the best fighter of the 1950s, the Hawker Hunter was also one of the most important combat aircraft of its era. The fact that it was Britain's first genuinely transonic operational aircraft was almost incidental in the light of its suitability for many roles, and it gained a popularity among more than a dozen national air forces which far outstripped the production run of fewer than 2000.

The aesthetics of the Hunter were probably responsible for more air force recruitment during its time in service than any other single factor. Nor were those pilots who made it into the frontline squadrons to fly the Hunter disappointed, rating it the jet equivalent of the Spitfire, right in every respect, elegant of line, strong almost to a fault and a delight to fly. Even an inexperienced pilot could safely handle this aeroplane at almost optimum performance, while in the hands of an expert it could be unmatched by anything else.

But its potential took some time to be realised and its development was marred by setbacks, some of the problems persisting well into RAF squadron service. The airbrake arrangement was arrived at by experimentation and in its final position it was damaged by spent ammunition links which then had to be collected in bulged excrescences, while pitch and longitudinal control were problems at high speed and firing the guns at altitude caused the engine to surge and flame out. All these and other difficulties

were eventually solved, but the Hunter's debut was less than auspicious.

Its origins go back to 1946 when the need for a Gloster Meteor replacement was already recognised, and early in 1947 Specification F.43/46 was issued for a single-seat interceptor to deal with high-speed bombers at high altitudes. Sydney (later Sir Sydney) Camm and his Hawker design team improved on that with a private venture, the P.1067 designed around the new Rolls-Royce AJ.65 axial flow turbojet, later known as the Avon as the company named its jet engines after rivers in the UK. Specification F.3/48 was issued in March 1948 to cover the new design and test pilot Neville Duke flew the first prototype from Boscombe Down in July 1951.

Of conventional construction, the Hunter had swept wings and tail, wing-root air intakes for its single engine and a demountable gun pack which was winched up into the fuselage, with the ammunition boxes behind the cockpit and the four 30 mm Aden guns beneath. The familiar problem of fuel storage for the thirsty jet engine led to early models being useful only as short-range interceptors, but the wings were modified and strengthened to take a variety of stores on strong points. In addition to drop tanks, rockets or 1000 pound bombs on the inner pylons, the Hunter could carry more rockets or retarded bombs under the outer wings.

Later models also had a dogtooth leading edge as an aerodynamic refinement to take advantage of the more powerful Avon 203 which produced more than 10,000 pounds of thrust. Camm had never liked the idea of afterburning, preferring a more powerful basic engine, and the Hunter's popularity with its pilots showed the wisdom of the principle. It was unusual in having no airframe limitations, easily exceeding Mach 1 in a dive although maximum level speed was Mach 0.95, and the airbrake could be used at any speed.

Hunters were used by the RAF's Black Arrow and Blue Diamond aerobatic teams and were export-ed to numerous countries. Licensed production was undertaken in the Netherlands by Aviolanda and Fokker, and in Belgium by SABCA and Avions Fairey, but most notable was the amount of factory work as Hunters were retired from one air force, refurbished and exported to another. The company was said to have made a much larger profit from such work than it did from the original production.

And Hawker Hunters are still in demand. They are entering private use, but military arms continue to use them for such things as calibrating shipboard armament. Sydney Camm's enduring design is still as effective as it is good-looking, half a century later.

One of the last operators of the Hawker Hunter was the Swiss Air Force which used the type initially as a fighter and later mainly in the ground attack role. These two Mk 58s were photographed near Emmen during October 1989. Visible under the forward fuselage are two of the Aden cannon ports and the fairing to contain the used ammunition links. *Gordon Bain*

• Hawker Hunter F Mk 6	
Manufacturer:	Hawker Aircraft Company
Type:	Single-seat fighter
Engine:	One Rolls-Royce Avon 207 axial flow turbojet, 10,150 lb s.t.
Wingspan:	33 ft 8 in .... 10.25 m
Length:	45 ft 10½ in .... 13.98 m
Height:	13 ft 2 in .... 4.02 m
Empty weight:	14,122 lb .... 6405 kg
Max loaded:	23,800 lb .... 10,796 kg
Normal range:	526 miles .... 1052 km
Max range:	1900 miles .... 3058 km
Max speed:	
– sea level	715 mph .... 1150 km/h
– 36,000 ft	623 mph .... 1002 km/h
First flight:	20 July 1951
In production:	1953-1959

HAWKER HURRICANE

Unlike the contemporary Spitfire which had a monocoque construction fuselage, the Hurricane used 1920s-technology steel tube, liberally braced with wires as seen in the Alpine Fighter Collection's Mk I example, undergoing restoration to fly by Air New Zealand at Christchurch. *John King*

Britain's first monoplane fighter to enter service seems forever destined to take second place to its more glamorous contemporary, the Spitfire. Slower, older in its construction techniques and showing more functionality than elegance in its line, the Hawker Hurricane has always been outshone by the Spitfire and survives to fly today in far fewer numbers.

But the Hurricane's place in aviation history must not be overlooked. Not only did the type serve in all theatres of World War 2 but it also bore the brunt of the Battle of Britain. Far more Hurricanes than Spitfires were in service with the RAF at that desperate time in the summer and autumn of 1940, and they scored a greater number of victories to keep Germany at bay.

Like many other notable warplanes, the Hurricane was conceived as a private venture. Sydney Camm first designed it as a Fury monoplane with enclosed cockpit, fixed undercarriage and a Rolls-Royce Goshawk engine, and it shared the earlier biplane Fury/Hart etc

series' well-established principles of a rigidly braced structure of steel and light alloy tubing with fabric covering. While that resulted in an airframe less aerodynamically efficient than a monocoque structure, the Hurricane was able to absorb punishment and, although slower than its Bf 109 opponent, could out-turn it and hold its own in a dogfight.

While still on the drawing board the new fighter received the more powerful PV-12 (later renamed the Merlin) engine and retracting gear, and a stressed-skin all-metal wing was being designed at an early stage. Another first was the provision of the unprecedented number of eight machine guns, mounted in the wings, and the Air Ministry wrote specification F.36/34 around the new fighter. So promising were the prototype flight tests that the huge quantity (for peacetime Britain) of 600 was ordered in June 1936, and by the time war was declared with Germany almost 500 had been delivered to equip 18 squadrons. Less than a year later, at the start of the Battle of Britain, the 2309 Hurricanes delivered outnumbered Spitfires by almost a thousand, and the Gloster factory was putting them out at the rate of 130 a month. By September 1944, when the last Hurricane emerged from the assembly lines, 14,231 had been made, 1451 of them in Canada.

As well as equipping the RAF and the Fleet Air Arm, the Hurricane also served with the air forces of Australia, Belgium, Canada, Egypt, the Netherlands, USSR, Finland, France, India, Iran, Romania, Ireland, South Africa, Turkey, Poland, New Zealand and Yugoslavia. The New Zealand examples were delivered to No. 488 Squadron in Singapore to replace the inadequate Brewster Buffaloes, just in time to be overrun by the Japanese, and a dozen Mk I Hurricanes went to help Finland in its 1939 Winter War with the Soviet Union, after which they were used against the Allies.

Hurricanes saw service in places Camm and his design team never envisaged when they first started

work on them in 1934. From the hot deserts of North Africa and the steamy tropical jungles of Asia and the western Pacific to the European Arctic, the Hurricane was popular with its pilots. Almost 3000 were delivered to the Soviet Union, where they operated on skis in winter, and today some are being retrieved for restoration from Arctic lakes and tundra, where they have lain for more than half a century.

The Hurricane was prominent in some desperate defence actions. The Battle of Britain was an even contest compared to the situation during the Malta convoy in August 1942, when 70 Sea Hurricanes fought off more than 600 enemy attackers, bringing down 39 of them for the loss of just seven of their own. In the gallantry of its pilots the Hurricane has earned a solid place in history. All too few remain in airworthy condition, but that situation is quietly being rectified in several countries.

Steve Johnson flies the Fighter Collection Hurricane out of Duxford. *Philip Makanna*

• Hawker Hurricane IIc		
Manufacturer:	........Hawker Aircraft Company	
Type:	......................Single-seat fighter/fighter-bomber	
Engine:	...................One Rolls-Royce Merlin XX V-12 cylinder, liquid cooled, 1280 hp	
Wingspan:	..............40 ft	........................12.19 m
Length:	....................32 ft 3 in	................9.83 m
Height:	...................13 ft 1 in	................4.0 m
Empty weight:	........5640 lb	...................2558 kg
Max loaded:	..........8250 lb	...................3742 kg
Normal range:	........460 miles	................740 km
Max range:	.............920 miles	................1480 km
Max speed:	.............335 mph	.................540 km/h at 18,000 ft
First flight:	..............6 November 1935	
In production:	1937-1944	

HAWKER SEA FURY

Howard Pardue bases and flies his Hawker Sea Fury out of Houston, Texas. *Philip Makanna*

In many respects Hawker's last piston-engine fighter was a direct parallel to the contemporary Grumman Bearcat. Both were designed in response to the idea that reliable engine power was not going to increase by much, so more performance depended on paring down size and particularly weight. The Fury and the Bearcat were their countries' ultimate – in both senses of the word – piston-engine fighters manufactured in quantity, and although they were too late to see action in World War 2, they played a significant part in the following conflict in Korea.

The German Focke-Wulfe Fw 190A had a great influence on fighter design thinking once it had been captured and examined by the British. Much smaller and with a loaded weight less than the Hawker Typhoon's empty weight, it had better manoeuvrability and a similar top speed with 600 hp less. Sydney Camm worked up a design for a smaller, lighter Tempest, eliminating the wing centre section and using a monocoque fuselage, a new feature for Hawker fighters.

Specification F.2/43 was drawn up in early 1943 around the project, and the requirement was pooled with N.7/43 for a carrier-based interceptor, with Hawker working on development of the land-based fighter and Boulton Paul Aircraft dealing with the naval version. The new Fury may have been the light-weight Tempest, but it still weighed 11,675 pounds loaded and its wing span was less than three feet shorter than its predecessor's. The three prototypes flew in the latter part of 1944 and early 1945 with a variety of engines, the Rolls-Royce Griffon 85 with contra-rotating propellers, Bristol Centaurus XII and XV, and Napier Sabre VII, the latter's 3055 hp giving a speed of 483 mph.

The end of World War 2 led to the cancellation of an order for 200 of each version, the first Sea Fury having flown without wing folding facilities in February 1945 and the fully navalised second prototype eight months later. With jet aircraft still an unknown quantity for carrier operation, however, the decision was made to proceed with the Sea Fury and the first example of the initial production batch of F Mk 10s flew in September 1946. Fifty were made for the Fleet Air Arm, powered by the 2550 hp Centaurus 18, before a change was made to the FB Mk 11 which supplemented the four 20 mm cannon with external stores.

Other versions included two-seat trainers as well as the FB Mk 51, with instruments in Dutch for the Royal Netherlands Navy which also operated 25 made under licence by Fokker. Of the total of 615 FB Mk 11s, which included some sub-variants, 101 flew with the Royal Australian Navy and were based aboard HMAS *Sydney* during the Korean War, and others went to the Royal Canadian Navy. Fifty-five land-based Furies, structurally capable of folding wings but without naval gear, went to the Iraqi Air Force and 87 similar aircraft to Pakistan, along with the second Fury prototype and five Sea Fury conversions. That was not the last of the exports, either, with 18 reconditioned fighters going to Burma and 15 to Cuba.

Hawker Furies and Sea Furies are still flown, but in private hands. Some of the Australian examples went to the USA where the type competes with success in the air races at Reno, but most of today's airworthy Furies came out of Iraq in the late 1970s.

• Hawker Sea Fury FB Mk 11		
Manufacturer:	........Hawker Aircraft Company	
Type:	......................Single-seat carrier-based fighter/fighter-bomber	
Engine:	....................One Bristol Centaurus 18 18-cylinder, air cooled, 2550 hp	
Wingspan:	..............38 ft 4¾ in..............11.69 m	
Length:	....................34 ft 8 in................10.56 m	
Height:	...................15 ft 10½ in............4.84 m	
Empty weight:	........9240 lb...................4191 kg	
Max loaded:	..........14,650 lb..................6645 kg	
Normal range:	........700 miles................1126 km	
Max range:	............1040 miles.............1674 km	
Max speed:		
– 18,000 ft	................460 mph	..........740 km/h
– 30,000 ft	................415 mph	................668 km/h
First flight:	..............1 September 1944	
In production:	1946-1950	

Six years of hard work, diplomacy, discretion, expertise and ship-chartering on the part of Ed Jurist and David Tallichet led to the arrival in Florida of some 27 airframes as an enormous jigsaw puzzle of fuselages, engines and wings, plus a second shipload of spare parts. From there they were sold to warbirds enthusiasts in several countries, including Australia as a coals-to-Newcastle exercise to join four ex-RAN Sea Furies still extant there. They have all needed a full strip and rebuild to clean them of the desert dust, but fully restored and mostly painted in ex-RAN colours they are one of the most popular warbird fighters, pleasant to fly and packing plenty of performance.

This Royal Australian Navy marked Hawker Sea Fury has been owned for over 25 years by Ellsworth Getchell, a former L1011 Captain with TWA, and is based at Hollister, California. *Gordon Bain*

LOCKHEED P-38 LIGHTNING

Philip Makanna

Radical and unorthodox, the twin-engine fighter which Lockheed produced at the beginning of 1939 had a number of things against it. The company, which had been through some corporate changes and collapses since Allan and Malcolm Loughead first started trading under their own name in 1916, had produced a number of trend-setting and successful transport aircraft but never anything in quantity for the military.

Apart from the layout of the twin booms, some technical innovations raised a few eyebrows, and what sort of fighter had a control wheel instead of an honest stick for the pilot? The Allison engines were untried and the turbochargers and engine coolant radiators, well behind the engines, were thought to be exposed and unnecessarily vulnerable. Brake fade caused the prototype XP-38 to fall into a ditch during initial taxiing trials, and despite continuing minor problems during the first four test flights it was flown on 11 February 1939 from March Field, California, to Mitchell Field, New York. The transcontinental flight took just over seven hours and the total elapsed time was only 15 minutes outside the existing record set by Howard Hughes in his H-1 racer, but loss of power on approach caused the XP-38's destruction by undershooting into a golf course, fortunately without injury to test pilot Lieutenant Ben Kelsey, USAAC project officer.

It was not a good start for reliability, but the P-38 went on to become the only American fighter to be in production both when the USA entered the war and also on VJ Day. More than 10,000 were built in an array of 18 variants, the final one of which, the P-38L, could carry 10 rockets or 4000 pounds of bombs under emergency power, and formations of P-38 bombers were led by droop-snoot lead ships with a navigator/bomb aimer in the nose. Others were fitted with radar as two-seat night fighters and even operated on skis or as fast aerial ambulances, able to carry two stretchers.

Lockheed's design team, led by Hall Hibbard, had come a close second to Bell in a 1936 multi-seat bomber destroyer competition, and the company was invited to participate, along with five others, in the design contest X-608 of 1938 which called for a twin-engine high-altitude interceptor. Kelly Johnson studied a number of layouts and settled on the now-familiar twin booms, each housing one 1150 hp Allison V-1710C, main undercarriage leg and exhaust-driven turbo-supercharger. The propellers were handed, rotating in different directions to counteract torque effects, and a central nacelle housed the pilot, nosewheel and armament of four 0.5 inch machine guns and a 23 mm Masden cannon, later replaced by a 20 mm Hispano cannon with twice as much ammunition.

European interest resulted in an export order even before the first USAAC deliveries. In April 1940 the Anglo-French Purchasing Committee ordered 667, but without turbochargers and handed propellers, against Lockheed's advice. Two sides to the story say either those countries' air arms wanted to standardise on the engines used in their P-40s for the medium-altitude combat then taking place, or else the US State Department refused to allow the export of turbocharged engines. When France fell to the Germans two months later the entire contract was diverted to the RAF, which refused delivery of what it considered to be a substandard product, although

• Lockheed P-38L Lightning

Manufacturer:	........Lockheed Aircraft Corporation	
Type:	......................Single-seat long-range escort fighter	
Engines:	.................Two Allison V-1710-111/113 V-12 cylinder, liquid cooled, 1425 hp	
Wingspan:	..............52 ft	........................15.86 m
Length:	....................37 ft 10 in	..............11.53 m
Height:	....................12 ft 10 in	..............3.9 m
Empty weight:	........14,100 lb	................6394 kg
Max loaded:	..........17,500 lb	................7936 kg
Normal range:	........460 miles	...............740 km
Max range:	............2260 miles	.............3560 km
Max speed:		
– 5000 ft	...................360 mph	.................580 km/h
– 15,000 ft	...............390 mph	.................628 km/h
First flight:	..............27 January 1939	
In production:	1941-1945	

it did provide the Lightning name which stuck.

But things improved and the P-38 was used in Europe, North Africa and the Pacific as a most effective long-distance bomber escort or ground attack aircraft. In the Pacific it was credited with the destruction of more Japanese aircraft than any other type and 16 P-38s intercepted the G4M Betty bomber carrying Admiral Yamamoto, 500 miles from their Guadalcanal base.

Its size precluded its use in close-combat dogfighting, but the Lockheed Lightning was one of the best of all long-range interceptors and escort fighters. Its range, reliability and multi-role capabilities put it at the forefront of Allied World War 2 aircraft.

Unconventional and at first controversial, the P-38 was an effective escort fighter despite its large wingspan. Denny Ghiringhelli flies the Lone Star Lightning near Galveston, Texas. Philip Makanna

MESSERSCHMITT BF 109

Hans Dittes' Bf 109G-10 was the star attraction at the 1996 Warbirds Over Wanaka airshow, and is being taxied here by Mark Hanna after assembly. *John King*

By far the most significant German combat aircraft of World War 2, and one of the greatest fighters of all time, was at first dismissed as inferior by the optimistic Allied forces. But that merely repeated the German commanders' initial reaction to the sight of Willy Messerschmitt's design when it first flew in May 1935 – small enough to look like a racing monoplane and powered by a British engine, the 695 hp Rolls-Royce Kestrel, it looked nothing like a fighter.

If history has taught us nothing else, it has shown how wrong first impressions can be. Messerschmitt's design, the first all-metal stressed-skin monoplane fighter with enclosed cockpit and retractable undercarriage to enter service, went on to be produced in greater quantities than any other combat aircraft while shooting down about twice as many of its opposition. Bf 109s comprised some 60 per cent of Germany's total fighter production, and by 1956, when the last of the Rolls-Royce Merlin engined HA-1112 version emerged from the Spanish factory in Seville, some 35,000 had been made during a production life of more than 20 years.

The Spanish connection started early in the Bf 109's career. In 1937 the German Kondor Legion was equipped with a small number of early production examples, which were so superior to anything else fighting in the Spanish Civil War, the He 51 biplanes having been unequal to the Republicans' Polikarpov I-16s, that they made a tremendous impression.

Some 200 Bf 109Es took part in the German invasion of Poland in September 1939 and shot down large numbers of defending PZL P.11c gull-winged monoplane fighters, but they finally met their match in the Spitfire during the Battle of Britain a year later. On the Eastern Front against the Soviet Union, however, the Bf 109 scored its highest number of kills, with Major Erich Hartmann credited with a confirmed 352 victories in his Bf 109G-14.

Continuous development saw the Messerschmitt fighter gain weight, power and armament. The first production version, the Bf 109B, was powered by a 720 hp Jumo 210Da inverted V-12 engine and had two 7.9 mm machine guns, an empty weight of 3483 pounds and maximum speed of 292 mph. The C model had slightly more power and two more guns, but the Bf 109E was the definitive version. From the outset provision had been made for the Daimler-Benz DB600 series of inverted V-12 engines, and the 1175 hp of the DB601A gave a speed of 348 mph for a weight of 4189 pounds, which by now included cannon in the wings and machine guns above the engine. The F had more power and an even smaller rudder, but the Bf 109G (Gustav), which was made in the greatest numbers, weighed around 6000 pounds empty with its bigger 1475 hp DB605 engine which gave it a top speed of 386 mph and landing characteristics described as "malicious".

The Bf 109 always demanded careful attention from its pilots, with its narrow-track undercarriage which could induce severe swing on takeoff or landing, and confined cockpit with systems such as manually wound flaps which typically took more than 20 seconds to extend. But it was a highly effective fighter, better than almost anything else at the time, which won air superiority over many countries and formed the mainstay of the Luftwaffe's fighter force.

Very few have survived, especially with the Daimler-Benz engine which gave it the characteristic pugnacious nose. A number of Spanish-produced examples still fly with Merlin engines and were seen in quantity in the film *The Battle of Britain*, but ironically the fighter made in the greatest numbers is now one of the rarest of them all.

One Bf 109G-2 was captured, damaged but intact, by No. 3 Squadron RAAF near Tobruk in October 1942 and was sent to Lydda in Palestine for performance assessment as it was the first of the new Gustav series to be captured by the Allies. Shipped to England, it made brief public appearances from storage, but in 1973 work was started to restore it to flying. "Black 6", still owned by the Ministry of Defence but registered G-USTV, flew again in March 1991, wearing its original North Africa colour scheme, and is seen here with Dave Southwood in the cockpit in July 1993. It was operated by the Imperial War Museum Duxford for display at airshows, initially for a period of three years but with an extension to five years, but on its last planned display flight, in October 1997, it was damaged in a forced landing at Duxford. *Philip Makanna*

• Messerschmitt Bf 109G-6		
Origin:	Bayerische Flugzeugwerke	
Type:	Single-seat fighter	
Engine:	One Daimler-Benz DB605AM inverted V-12, liquid-cooled, 1475 hp	
Wingspan:	32 ft 6½ in	9.92 m
Length:	29 ft 0½ in	8.85 m
Height:	8 ft 2½ in	2.50 m
Empty weight:	5893 lb	2673 kg
Max loaded:	6945 lb	3150 kg
Normal range:	450 miles	725 km
Max speed:		
– sea level	340 mph	547 km/h
– 22,640 ft	386 mph	621 km/h
First flight:	September 1935	
In production:	1937-1944 (to 1956 by Hispano Aviación)	

Mitsubishi A6M Rei-sen (Zero-sen)

Airworthy Japanese fighters of World War 2 are among the rarest of warbirds. Randy Wilson is at the controls of the Confederate Air Force's Zero. *Philip Makanna*

Many countries which fought in World War 2 had fighter aircraft which their people closely identified with. Britain had the Spitfire, the Americans the Mustang or perhaps the Lightning, and Germany had the Messerschmitt 109, all excellent aircraft and symbolic of their gallant pilots' efforts.

For the Japanese, that representative fighter was the Rei-sen, a contraction of the official designation Type 0 (it was put into production in 1940, the Japanese year 5700) Carrier Fighter or Rei shiki Kanjo sentoki, better known to the rest of the world as the Zero although its official Allied code name was Zeke. It was denigrated by the Allied propaganda machine, which overlooked the success of its immediate predecessors in the Sino-Japanese War of 1937 as well as the Zero's own superiority in China in 1940. Those operations were reported with some urgency by General Claire Chennault, commander of the the American Volunteer Group the Flying Tigers, but ignored by the bureaucrats in Washington.

The Zero was a carrier-borne fighter capable of mixing it with the best of its Western land-based opponents, at least until mid-1943. The nearly 11,000 made by Mitsubishi and Nakajima played a major role in the Pacific war which was sparked when more than 400 of the previously ignored Zero, plus other types, pounced on Pearl Harbor in the early morning of 7 December 1941 with such devastating effect. For 18 months the Zero reigned supreme in southeast Asia and the Pacific.

In May 1937 the Imperial Navy Staff issued an outline specification for a successor to the A5M shipboard fighter. Mitsubishi assigned the project to Jiro Horikoshi's team, which had been responsible for the A5M and came up with an all-metal fighter with retractable undercarriage, powered by a 780 hp Mitsubishi MK2 Zuisei radial engine which gave it a top speed of 316 mph. Agility was always an important aspect of any Japanese design, and the A6M achieved that with light weight, minimal armour and careful attention to aerodynamic detail. Armament was two 20 mm cannon in the wings and a pair of 7.7 mm machine guns above the forward fuselage.

More power, in the form of the 950 hp Nakajima NK1C Sakae 12 or later 1130 hp Sakae 21, boosted the performance to around 350 mph. Part of the Zero's mystique – which rapidly built up once the Allies had officially recognised its existence and potential – was its range. The modest engine was economical on fuel, and internal tankage of 156 gallons could be supplemented by drop tanks to give an endurance of six to eight hours, which allowed formations of Zeros to attack targets otherwise considered to be safely out of range. Bombs could also be carried on wing racks.

Adding to its versatility in parts of the Pacific Ocean islands where airfields were hard to develop, as well as acting as a convoy escort, was a floatplane version. The A6M2-N was made in Koizumi by Nakajima and reached 273 mph with its single central float and pair of underwing stabiliser floats, but it was never fully effective as a fighter.

Lack of development of its planned successors led to some evolution of the Zero in the latter war years, and the A6M8 was the final product which never reached beyond the prototype stage. Armour plating and self-sealing tanks were provided, the wings were strengthened to carry a heavier bomb load and the engine was upgraded to the 1560 hp Mitsubishi Kinsei 62, which left no room for fuselage armament but boosted the top speed to 360 mph.

In many ways the Zero-sen's fortunes paralleled those of Japan itself. Invincible at the outset and superior to anything the Allies could put up against it, the fighter was incapable of any real development and was overtaken by the later output of the American aircraft industry. Few examples remain of this carrier-borne fighter which was the terror of the Pacific and became Japan's best and most famous of all warplanes.

Light and highly manoeuvrable, the Zero was at first invincible in the Pacific theatre until the Allies adopted different tactics. The Planes of Fame Zero catches the setting sun near its base at Chino, California. *Philip Makanna*

• Mitsubishi A6M3 Rei-sen (Zero-sen)	
Manufacturer:	Mitsubishi Jukogyo Kabushiki Kaisha
Type:	Single-seat naval fighter
Engine:	One Nakajima NK1C Sakae 21 14-cylinder radial, air cooled, 1130 hp
Wingspan:	39 ft 4½ in .... 12.0 m
Length:	29 ft 8¾ in .... 9.06 m
Height:	9 ft 8 in .... 2.98 m
Empty weight:	4107 lb .... 1863 kg
Max loaded:	5906 lb .... 2679 kg
Normal range:	1160 miles .... 1866 km
Max range:	1930 miles .... 3105 km
Max speed:	336 mph .... 541 km/h at 20,000 ft
First flight:	1 April 1939
In production:	1940-1945

NORTH AMERICAN P-51 MUSTANG

This P-51A was flown new to Ladd Field, Alaska, for use by the Cold Weather Test Detachment, but crashed in heavy snow in 1944. The remains were recovered in 1977 by Walden Spillers, and rebuilt in Ohio.

Being an A model P-51, *Polar Bear* is powered by an Allison V1710-85 driving a three-blade Curtiss Electric propeller. Essentially it is a full-blown P-51A, but the radiator has been replaced with one from a P-51D. *Gordon Bain*

The Americans regard the P-51 Mustang in much the same way as the British do the Spitfire – with a great deal of respect, even warmth, and with a willingness to defend the type against all detractors, real or imagined. They make a case, and a very strong case, for the Mustang having been the best all-round fighter of World War 2, showing an excellence which kept it in military service for many years afterwards.

The ironical thing about the excellence and popularity of this American fighter is that it was developed to a British specification. Without the British initiative the company of North American Aviation, which had so far produced only trainers with varying degrees of aggression, might never have had the chance to show what it could do.

By 1939 the British were seriously regretting their 1930s policy of "peace in our time" in the face of massive German re-armament, and had to make up the numbers. Desperately seeking another front-line fighter, the British Purchasing Commission visited the USA to arrange rapid production of the Curtiss Hawk 87, better known as the P-40. Advised to approach

another manufacturer with spare production capacity not tied up in American contracts, the commission called on "Dutch" Kindelberger, chairman of North American Aviation, who said his company could do even better.

The story that North American designed, built and test flew its NA-73X within 17 weeks is part of aviation lore, but it's not quite the full story. The company cheated slightly, in that it had already been working on a private venture, a high-performance fighter based on the P-40 which had originally been designed with a ventral radiator. Adding several years' research from various sources – including the laminar-flow wing, not originally envisaged for the Mustang project – and incorporating them all into their own design which used some existing or beefed-up systems from the AT-6, the designers came up with an outstanding aircraft.

Fractionally bigger than the Spitfire and with similar power from its Allison engine, the new Mustang had heavier firepower, three times the fuel capacity and a higher speed. Down low, that is, for the Allison lacked the supercharger punch for higher altitudes, and the early P-51 and A-36 Invader, built because more American money was available for such aircraft than for pursuit fighters, were used as low-level attack fighter-bombers.

In 1942 the company agreed that installation of a Rolls-Royce Merlin might be a good idea, and a considerable rework resulted in the P-51B, highly successful and everything that anybody could ask for. With an extra fuel tank behind the pilot and drop tanks under the wings, it had a range of more than 2000 miles and could escort bomber formations deep into German-occupied Europe. If enemy fighters were encountered, the tanks were jettisoned and the Mustang could deal on even terms with Bf 109s and Fw 190s.

Altogether 15,586 Mustangs were produced, including 266 made in Australia by the Commonwealth Aircraft Corporation. The definitive model was the P-51D with 1590 hp licence-built Packard Merlin engine,

• North American P-51D Mustang		
Manufacturer:	........North American Aviation Inc.	
Type:	......................Single-seat fighter	
Engine:	...................One Packard Merlin V-1650-7 V-12 cylinder, liquid cooled, 1450 hp	
Wingspan:	..............37 ft 0½ in	..............11.29 m
Length:	...................32 ft 2½ in	..............9.81 m
Height:	...................13 ft 8 in	.................4.1 m
Empty weight:	........7635 lb	...................3462 kg
Max loaded:	..........11,600 lb	.................5260 kg
Normal range:	........950 miles	...............1530 km
Max range:	...........1650 miles	..............2655 km
Max speed:		
– 5,000 ft	.................395 mph	.................636 km/h
– 25,000 ft	...............437 mph	.................703 km/h
First flight:	..............26 October 1940	
In production:	1941-1945	

cut-down rear fuselage and teardrop canopy for rearward vision, and it saw service mainly in the European theatre and, in RAAF hands made locally under licence, in the Pacific. After that came the P-51K and the lightweight P-51H, an extensively redesigned Mustang with 2218 hp Merlin which gave it a top speed not far short of 500 mph.

After the war the Mustang was still popular, serving with 55 air forces as the standard piston-engine fighter-bomber into the era of the jets. It saw extensive use in Korea, and in 1967 was back in production by Cavalier as the Turbo Mustang III and the Piper Enforcer.

Given its good handling qualities and robust build, the Mustang is highly popular as a warbird, currently flying in higher numbers than any other fighter and in all countries where the movement is active.

P-51D *Huntress III* is owned and flown by Robert Converse of Bakersfield, California. *Philip Makanna*

POLIKARPOV I-16 ISHAK

Test flying a tricky new type involves much discussion, as seen at Wanaka in October 1997 with Tom Middleton (left), Mark Hanna and, in the cockpit, Grant Bissett.
John King

Short and stubby, with a close-coupled, barrel-shaped fuselage which suggested its designer had been influenced by the Granville brothers' Gee Bee series of racers of the early 1930s, the Polikarpov I-16 was hard to take seriously at first. It was ignored by aviation analysts when it first appeared, fighting on the Republican side in the Spanish Civil War, but it soon proved highly effective, nicknamed Mosca (fly) by its pilots and Rata (rat) by its opponents.

The Russian fighter was a remarkable aeroplane, far in advance of anything the West was making when it first flew in 1933. At a time when all combat aircraft were biplanes, with built-in headwinds caused by struts, wires and undercarriage, here was something with cantilever monoplane wings, variable pitch propeller and retractable undercarriage, well-armed with two rapid-firing machine guns and two cannon, and boasting excellent performance. It had some short-comings, particularly in ground handling, and it certainly lacked elegance of line, but the I-16 Ishak (little donkey) was outstandingly manoeuvrable, with a high rate of roll and a climb rate second to none.

Nikolai Polikarpov was already known for his range of biplane fighters when he put the I-16 to pencil. As with other examples of Russian technology, it was designed for mass production by semi-skilled workers and able to be maintained in the field under harsh climatic conditions. The centre section was built up of tubular steel and the wings were fabric covered metal, but the strong fuselage structure was wooden, using thin strips of beech veneer, three layers thick, laid over a former. The open cockpit was snug around the shoulders and the gear was hand-cranked by a cable winch between the pilot's feet which, combined with extremely sensitive controls, could make life interesting at times.

Early versions were powered by a 480 hp modified Bristol Jupiter radial, but most had various models of the Shvetsov radial engine derived from the Wright Cyclone, culminating in the Type 24 with 1000 hp M-62R. About 8600 examples of all models were made, including two-seat trainers with tandem open cockpits, and the I-16 was the most numerous Soviet fighter until 1943.

As well as its introduction in Spain, fighting against the Nationalist forces which were gaining operational experience for the forthcoming World War 2, the Polikarpov was used against Japanese aircraft over China and Manchuria. About half the production was engaged against German invading forces in Russia after 1941, although it was outclassed by the more modern German fighters and its continued development held back the introduction of more modern (and less tricky) Soviet fighters.

Some early examples lasted in Spanish use as late as 1952, but otherwise the I-16 faded from view. Until the 1990s, that is.

Their reappearance on the world warbird scene is due to the availability of aircraft from the former Eastern Bloc. The wreckages of desirable military aircraft, lying where they had fallen in the vastness of Soviet Russia during the prolonged and intense fighting, caught the attention of warbird collectors, but New Zealand's Sir Tim Wallis realised the significance of some of the lesser known types, and so began his Polikarpov project.

• Polikarpov I-16 Ishak		
Manufacturer:	........TsKB (Central Design Bureau)	
Type:	......................Single-seat fighter	
Engine:	...................One Shetsov M-62 9-cylinder radial, air cooled, 1000 hp	
Wingspan:	..............29 ft 6¾ in	..............9.0 m
Length:	...................20 ft 1¾ in	..............6.125 m
Height:	...................8 ft 4¾ in	.................2.56 m
Empty weight:	........3370 lb	....................1528 kg
Max loaded:	..........4215 lb	....................1912 kg
Normal range:	........250 miles	...............402 km
Max range:	............435 miles	...............700 km
Max speed:	...........326 mph	.................525 km/h
First flight:	..............31 December 1933	
In production:	1935-1942	

He already had business contacts in Russia and saw the restoration of crashed aircraft as a way to utilise the moribund aircraft factories, particularly in Siberia where wartime production had originally been established to escape the conflict further west. The existing design bureaux had all the expertise and, even more importantly, all the original design data and drawings, so the restoration of six Polikarpov I-16s and three I-153 biplanes was undertaken, some to be retained by the Alpine Fighter Collection and others to be sold later.

Their public debut, at Warbirds Over Wanaka in April 1998, was the first time a formation of I-16s had been seen together for decades and was a highly popular part of the airshow.

Mark Hanna (front), Steve Taylor, Keith Skilling and John Lamont are still getting used to the Alpine Fighter Collection's Polikarpov I-16s, although the formation work would suggest otherwise during the 1998 Warbirds Over Wanaka airshow. *Philip Makanna*

REPUBLIC P-47 THUNDERBOLT

Philip Makanna

The sheer bulk of the Thunderbolt, World War 2's largest and heaviest single-engine fighter, disguises the company's original ideas of a fast, lightweight pursuit aircraft. But times and minds change, and with them the concept of combat aircraft.

The Seversky Aircraft Corporation under chief designer Alexander Kartveli had from 1935 produced a number of neat radial-engine fighters including the P-35. The line culminated in the P-43 as the company changed its name in 1939 to Republic Aviation Corporation, and the next projects, the XP-47 and XP-47A ordered in January 1940, were to be powered by the V-12 liquid cooled Allison V-1710. The result would be fighters which combined high speed with light weight.

But that specification was cancelled and replaced by the XP-47B which, despite the similarity in type number, had nothing to do with the earlier XP-47s. The new contract called for a large and heavily armed fighter to be designed around the new 2000 hp Pratt & Whitney R-2800 Double Wasp, sprouting eight 0.5 inch machine guns from the wings. Kartveli's solution to the problem of location of the large turbocharger was to install it in the bottom of the rear fuselage, with the necessarily long exhaust pipes

passing back under the elliptical wing and the compressed air ducts above it, forward to the carburettor. Between them, below the cockpit floor, were the fuel tanks.

The large engine needed a large propeller to absorb the power, even with the unprecedented number of four blades. That led to its own problems with the length of the inwards-folding undercarriage legs which still had to leave room in the outer wings for the guns, plus their ammunition troughs extending almost to the wing tips. Even after the prototypes of the massive fighter were flying, numerous and protracted technical problems had to be overcome, not least among them engine failures, crashes and inadequate climb performance and manoeuvrability. The P-47C had the engine mounted eight inches further forward, plus a redesigned rudder and elevator balance system, and the first production orders were received in September 1941.

Republic's P-47 went on to be made in large numbers. Of the 15,660 built over three and a half years, no fewer than 12,602 were bubble-canopied P-47Ds, more than any other fighter sub-type. Nicknamed the 'Jug', the P-47 had such a roomy fuselage that one joker said that if he was shot at and needed to take evasive action, all he had to do was undo his straps and run around inside the cockpit. The reality was, however, that the cockpit was so cluttered with equipment that he would soon have tripped.

Despite its size, the Thunderbolt was a respected fighter, particularly at high altitude. Its value and range increased further with the development of hard points to carry drop tanks, and it was able to escort bombers all the way to their targets deep inside Europe and back. Resilience and fire power were its forte and, coupled with the ability to achieve 550 mph in a terminal dive, made it the equal of any Axis fighter.

With stiffened wings able to carry external stores such as rockets or two 1000 pound bombs, the P-47 was a formidable attack aircraft. It was used as such

• Republic P-47D Thunderbolt		
Manufacturer:	........Republic Aviation Corporation	
Type:	......................Single-seat fighter/fighter-bomber	
Engine:	..................One Pratt & Whitney R-2800-59 Double Wasp 18-cylinder radial, air cooled, 2300 hp	
Wingspan:	.............40 ft 9½ in	..............12.4 m
Length:	..................36 ft 1½ in	..............11.03 m
Height:	..................14 ft 2 in	................4.3 m
Empty weight:	........10,700 lb	................4853 kg
Max loaded:	..........19,400 lb	................8800 kg
Normal range:	........560 miles	..............900 km
Max range:	............1800 miles	..............2896 km
Max speed:		
– 5000 ft	................363 mph	................584 km/h
– 25,000 ft	...............428 mph	................689 km/h
First flight:	..............6 May 1941	
In production:	1942-1945	

before, during and after the Allied invasion of France and the advance eastwards across Europe, as well as by the RAF in the Far East and by the Soviet Union under Lend-Lease. The faster, lightweight P-47M with 2800 hp engine was used against the German jets, and the N model with bigger wings and more fuel capacity was able to escort B-29s on raids over Japan.

The 'Jug' stayed in service with the USAF and a number of other countries' air arms for several years after World War 2, although not to the same extent as the Mustang. In terms of size, speed and sheer weight of numbers it was hard to overlook, but the P-47 was more than just a massive fighter and earned a great deal of respect from its users.

Tarheel Hal is the Lone Star's P-47D, flown here by Tom Gregory out of Houston, Texas. *Philip Makanna*

SUPERMARINE SPITFIRE

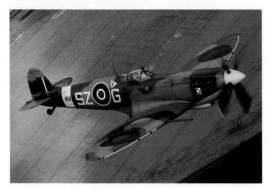

Rolf Meum flies the Old Flying Machine Company's Mk IX Spitfire near its Duxford base. *Philip Makanna*

Of all the combat aircraft of World War 2, the Spitfire has attracted the most attention. More words, most of them eulogistic, have been written about this famous fighter than any other.

Very little of that is criticism. True, it was difficult to manufacture in quantity and needed care in its ground handling with its narrow-track undercarriage and lack of forward visibility. The Spitfire also lacked range in its original form, but it was designed at a time when fighters were intended for close home defence. Its elegance of line might have been surprising, coming from a company whose major output to date had been the ungainly but functional Walrus biplane amphibian, but the sleek Schneider Trophy race winners had given a hint of better ideas.

Reginald Mitchell, who did not live to see his creation enter RAF service, designed his Type 300 in 1934 in response to the lack of success of his prototype fighter Type 224, made to specification F.7/30 but hampered by its Rolls-Royce Goshawk engine. His combination of an elliptical wing, with NACA 2200 aerofoil section to give low drag, and Rolls-Royce PV-12 (later named the Merlin) engine was an inspired design based on sound technical development and gave the new Spitfire the edge in performance. American and German designers had been

using stressed-skin metal construction, particularly in their bombers and passenger aircraft, but the British predilection for fabric covering, often still with wooden structure, meant the new all-metal Supermarine fighter was revolutionary – and regarded with suspicion at first in some official circles.

The Spitfire was a private venture, far exceeding the revised F.5/34 specification which called for eight machine guns, enclosed cockpit and retractable undercarriage. It was submitted to the Air Ministry, which promptly wrote specification F.37/34 around it and in January 1935 accepted the design for prototype construction. On 5 March 1936 Vickers and Supermarine chief test pilot Mutt Summers took the new Spitfire for its first test flight, and an aviation legend was born.

Over a production period of 10 years nearly 23,000 Spitfires and navalised Seafires were made in 40 major variants, most of them in a specially constructed factory at Castle Bromwich near Birmingham. Constant development resulted in extra performance at the expense of twice the power and weight. When it first entered RAF service the Spitfire I weighed 5784 pounds fully loaded and had a maximum speed of 362 mph with its 1030 hp Merlin II engine. The final postwar Seafire F Mk 47, still with basically the same wing design and area, had a maximum weight of 12,530 pounds and a speed of 452 mph, powered by 2375 hp of Rolls-Royce Griffon 87 with contra-rotating propellers to avoid swing on takeoff.

Much of its appeal to the general public lies in the Spitfire's clean lines, for this is a fighter which has always looked right. Its first service period made it conspicuous, too, when it fought alongside the Hawker Hurricane in those early days of the war which culminated in the Battle of Britain. It was more than a match for the Messerschmitt Bf 109, its main adversary at that stage of the war, although the Spitfire needed development to be able to cope with the new Focke-Wulf Fw 190.

• Supermarine Spitfire LF XVIe	
Manufacturer:	Vickers Armstrong
Type:	Single-seat fighter
Engine:	One Packard Merlin V-1650-266 V-12 cylinder, liquid cooled, 1670 hp
Wingspan:	36 ft 10 in ....11.23 m
Length:	29 ft 11 in ....9.12 m
Height:	11 ft 5 in ....3.48 m
Empty weight:	5985 lb ....2714 kg
Max loaded:	8700 lb ....3945 kg
Normal range:	712 miles ....1146 km
Max speed:	416 mph ....670 km/h
First flight:	5 March 1936
In production:	1938-1947

Although the Spitfire was used mainly in Europe, it saw service in all major theatres of World War 2, particularly with the RAF and RAAF. Spitfires fought against the Japanese over Australia and Burma, and throughout the Solomon Islands, Borneo and New Guinea. They fought over the beaches during the Dunkirk evacuation and above the D-Day landings four years later, and today are among the most prized and valued of all active warbirds, appreciated by their pilots for their flying characteristics and by the public for their part in winning the war.

Spitfire evolution – Mk XVI (foreground, flown by Sir Tim Wallis) with 1720 hp Packard Merlin, and Mk XIV (Mark Hanna) with cut-down rear fuselage and 2050 hp Rolls-Royce Griffon, of the Alpine Fighter Collection over the high country near Lake Wanaka, New Zealand, in April 1994. Sir Tim was seriously injured in a takeoff crash in his Mk XIV in January 1996, but he is recovering and the Spitfire is being rebuilt. *John King*

YAKOVLEV YAK-1 TO YAK-9

Tiger Destefani flies his Yak-3 near Bakersfield, California. *Philip Makanna*

Even before entering the Shukovski Aviation Academy in 1927, Aleksandir Sergeivich Yakovlev had won a design competition for a light sporting aircraft. His subsequent career with Polikarpov suffered a setback when one of his designs lost an aileron, but earnest discussions with Stalin led to a chance to design a fighter. The Soviet UV-VS, Upravlenie Voenno-vozdushnikh Sily, or Administration of the Air Force, called for single-seat "frontal" and high-altitude fighters in 1938, and Yakovlev offered his Ya-26 and Ya-28 proposals which were accepted and designated I-26 and I-28.

The I-26 prototype flew in January 1940. Its compact design and liquid cooled Klimov V-12 engine, at first the 1100 hp M-105 developed from the Hispano-Suiza 12Ycrs and later the two-stage supercharged 1240 hp M-105PF, set the scene for all the piston-engine Yakovlev fighters which followed. It also made Yakovlev's name as a pre-eminent Soviet aircraft designer. By the end of 1940 more than 60 pre-series and production I-26s had been made and the designation was changed to Yak-1, cleared for production as the chief Soviet fighter. The wings were made of wood and contained the fuel tanks, while the welded steel-tube fuselage had an aluminium covering over the forward section and fabric-covered plywood skinning aft.

A 20 mm ShVAK cannon fired through the propeller spinner and two synchronised 7.62 mm ShKAS machine guns were mounted just forward of the cockpit.

As the Germans advanced into Russia the aircraft manufacturing plants were moved a thousand miles eastwards to Kamensk-Uralskii, beyond the Ural Mountains, but that led to only a minor hiccup in production. The urgent need for production outstripped facilities for development, but the Yak-1M (Modifikatsirovanny, or Modified) was given reduced wing span and area, plus lighter fuselage structure and lower rear decking for better pilot's view in combat. More power from a Klimov M-105PF-2 and relocating the oil cooler from the chin position to the wing root resulted in the Yak-3. The all-metal I-30 design of 1940 had also been designated Yak-3 but was discontinued in autumn 1941, but the Yak-3U, the last version of the Yak-1M-derived fighter with extra cannon, 1650 hp and all-metal construction, arrived too late to see World War 2 service.

Performance was helped by a thick coating of hard-wearing wax polish applied to the airframe, and in the Yak-3 the Germans realised they had met their match, directing Luftwaffe units on the Eastern Front to "avoid combat below 5000 metres with Yakovlev fighters lacking an oil cooler under the nose".

The original high-altitude I-28, or Yak-5, never reached production, and next to appear was the Yak-7. Originally a two-seat trainer version of the Yak-1, the Yak-7V had the Yak-1M improvements and was so successful that it was made in two major single-seat versions, the -7A night fighter with advanced radio equipment and the -7B day fighter. That was later supplanted by the Yak-9, a development of the Yak-7 which retained the plywood fuselage skin but had a metal spar which gave more room for fuel and overcame some of the type's range and endurance problems. Large numbers of Yak-9 variants were produced to fill all possible roles.

Fast, manoeuvrable, simple and rugged, the brilliant series of Yakovlev fighters were more than equal to anything flown by either side during World War 2. More than 37,000 were made, and the Yak-9 alone was made in higher numbers than any other Soviet combat aircraft except the Il-2 Shturmovik, remaining in service with Soviet and satellite air forces well into the 1950s.

No airworthy examples of that massive output remain, but recent production of Yak-3s and Yak-9s has been undertaken in the original factories, under the control of the Yakovlev Design Bureau headed by Sergei Yakovlev, son of the original designer. The original jigs and drawings are utilised, but as no useable Klimov engines are available the American Allison V-12, as seen in the P-40 series, is used instead. The Yakovlev lives on.

The first example of the new build Yak-9U to reach the USA was delivered to Eddie Andreini at Half Moon Bay, California, in late 1995. For the 1998 show season he had smoke generators fitted to the wingtips to provide a spectacular display. *Gordon Bain*

• Yakovlev Yak-9D	
Origin:	A.S. Yakovlev Design Bureau
Type:	Single-seat fighter
Engine:	One Klimov VK-105PF V-12 cylinder, liquid-cooled, 1260 hp
Wingspan:	30 ft 9¾ in .... 9.2 m
Length:	28 ft 0½ in .... 8.56 m
Height:	8 ft .... 2.44 m
Empty weight:	5269 lb .... 2390 kg
Max loaded:	6867 lb .... 3115 kg
Normal range:	840 miles .... 1350 km
Max speed:	
– sea level	332 mph .... 534 km/h
– 10,000 ft	374 mph .... 602 km/h
First flight:	June 1942
In production:	1942-1946

GUIDO ZUCCOLI GARDENS

These gardens are named after Guido Zuccoli a resident
of Toowoomba who made a significant contribution to
aviation in Australia and overseas. Mr Zuccoli's dedication
to his profession and life's work influenced the lives of many
people in a positive way.